Morgan Stanley

Wealth Management
215 Bluffs Ave Suite 100
Elko, NV 89801

Craig,

Thanks again for your support. I meant to give this to you when you were here but I forgot. I hope you enjoy.

Kurt

Kurt Neddenriep, CIMA®
The Mountain West Group at Morgan Stanley
Senior Portfolio Manager
Senior Vice President
Wealth Advisor
CA Insurance Lic. # 0C24092
www.morganstanleyfa.com/themountainwestgroup
kurt.neddenriep@morganstanley.com

Reno Office
5390 Kietzke Lane Ste 200
Reno, NV 89511
tel 888 434 3079

Combat Finance

How Military Values and Discipline Will Help You Achieve Financial Freedom

Craig,

Thank you so much for your friendship and support. I hope you enjoy this copy of Combat Finance.

Allons!

Kurt

Kurt Neddenriep

WILEY

Cover image: iStockphoto.com (Background: Andrey Kuzmin / Emblem: Grynold)
Cover design: Wiley

Published by John Wiley & Sons, Inc., Hoboken, New Jersey.
Published simultaneously in Canada.

For general information on our other products and services or for technical support, please contact our Customer Care Department within the United States at (800) 762-2974, outside the United States at (317) 572-3993 or fax (317) 572-4002.

Wiley publishes in a variety of print and electronic formats and by print-on-demand. Some material included with standard print versions of this book may not be included in e-books or in print-on-demand. If this book refers to media such as a CD or DVD that is not included in the version you purchased, you may download this material at http://booksupport.wiley.com. For more information about Wiley products, visit www.wiley.com.

Library of Congress Cataloging-in-Publication Data:

Neddenriep, Kurt.
Combat finance : how military values and discipline will help you achieve financial freedom / Kurt Neddenriep.
pages cm
Includes index.
ISBN 978-1-118-81750-6 (cloth); ISBN 978-1-118-81753-7 (ebk);
ISBN 978-1-118-81752-0 (ebk)
1. Finance, Personal. 2. Military discipline. I. Title.
HG179.N4136 2014
332.024--dc23

2013038601

Printed in the United States of America
10 9 8 7 6 5 4 3 2 1

To my beautiful wife, Katie, who has walked beside me
through two commands, a deployment,
and Combat Finance—*I love you, sweet girl.*
To the men and women of 1st squadron, 221st cavalry,
both past and present. Thank you for your
dedication, service, professionalism, and support.
It has truly been my honor to serve with you.
To SPC Brandon K. Steffey
and his military working dog Maci,
both KIA October 25, 2009, Laghman province, Afghanistan,
and to all of our fallen servicemen and -women.
May we live lives that are worthy of your sacrifice.

Contents

Preface

Combat Finance is a financial self-help book that takes the fog of the everyday financial battle and breaks it down into an easily understandable process that you can use to reach personal financial freedom. I think you'll find it to be an uplifting read that uses basic military analogies to help explain financial concepts in a way that you can immediately apply to your personal situation, regardless of whether you are 18 or 81. The purpose of this book is to both educate and entertain and, therefore, it is not a financial dissertation, nor is it a white paper on military doctrine and tactics. It is not a book of war stories about staring down the enemy and it's not just for those with military service. It is a book that will make sense even if the closest you have ever come to the military is making cookies with a Cub Scout den mother.

I wrote *Combat Finance* to help instill the values, principles, and discipline that it takes to succeed financially, so don't expect any gimmicks or get rich quick schemes. But don't get me wrong—getting your finances under control doesn't have to be like getting a root canal, either. You'll see that following the fundamentals and maintaining self-discipline is easy when you have a plan and a process. That is what I'm going to teach you in *Combat Finance,* and I think you're even going to have some fun along the way. Who knows, you might even learn to appreciate what you have more and worry about what you don't have less, all the while knowing that you have a plan in place to become wildly successful over time. After all, who wants to just get by? As a *Combat Finance* reader I want you to set high expectations for you and your family and then surpass those expectations. But to get there you need a plan, a process, and the discipline to see it through, so let's get going.

Acknowledgments

I am deeply grateful for the support, advice, and love of my family and friends, especially my wife Katie, who supports me in all my endeavors, both brilliant and not so. To my father, Doug, who taught me to never quit and my mother, Jean, who loved me no matter what. To Lizanne and Kristie for being the best big sisters a guy could ask for. Thanks to you two, I never had to face anything by myself growing up unless I chose to go it alone.

I would also like to add my sincere gratitude to the following:

John Mack, without whom this book would not have been published. Thank you for your years of support for our firm's military reservists. The men and women of the Wildhorse Squadron will never forget that you, and James Gorman flew all the way to Indianapolis to see us off on our deployment and never sought a word of recognition. Thank you both for making our firm a great place to work.

Eric Lupfer of William Morris Endeavor, I knew that the son of a retired armor officer would get results, and you did. Your advice and counsel have been a tremendous resource, and I cannot thank you enough.

My wealth advisory team, José Negrete, Deborah Marcom, Joel McConnell, and Ryan Gilbrech, as well as David Lawrence, David

Fritz, Curt Petersen, Nick Gormley, and Melissa Gutknecht. Thank you all for your support. I could not have done this without your efforts.

David Darst and Congressman Mark Amodei for your advanced praise for Combat Finance. Thank you for your trust and confidence.

Dr. Ty Cobb and Ted Stoever for your advice and unwavering friendship.

The men and women of the Wildhorse, 1-221 Armored Reconnaissance Squadron, both past and present. Your dedication, discipline, and professionalism will live with me for the rest of my life. It was an honor to serve with you and to command such a fine group of men and women.

Major General Frank Gonzales, Major General Giles Vanderhoof, Brigadier General Bob Fitch, Brigadier General William Burks, Colonel Jerry Bussel, Colonel Dennis George, Colonel John Morrow, Colonel Steve Spitze, Colonel Lou Cabrera, LTC Scott Cunningham, and all of the past commanders of the Nevada National Guard and the 1-221 ARS, thank you for your leadership and support. I could not have asked for a finer group of mentors.

Command Sergeant Major (CSM) Paul Kinsey for taking me under your wing as my squad leader when I enlisted as well as serving with distinction as my CSM during my last year of command. Who would have thought those two young grunts would be the command team some day? Thank you for teaching me how to take care of soldiers and their families.

Command Sergeant Major (CSM) James Richardson for your outstanding service as the first CSM of my command and for all of your support and friendship in Afghanistan. I could not have made it through without you. I would have fewer Bruce Springsteen and Celine Dion songs stuck in my head, but it would have been harder to bear the tough days.

Chaplain Hal Woomer for getting me through some of the darkest days of our deployment and Chaplains William Ohler and Aaron Oliver for their dedication to our cavalry troopers when we returned.

Master Chief Warrant Officer 5 David Anderson, Lieutenant Colonel Mike Glynn, Major Randy Lau, Major Blain Holmes, Major Doug Seymour, Captain Scott Adair, Captain Nick Soapes, Captain Nick Moran, Captain John Minnich, Captain Michael Schiemer,

Captain Patrick Arizmendi, Captain Joseph Claros, Captain Andrew Coughlan, Captain Thomas Hopper, Captain Paul Adcox, Captain Phil Gingrich, and Captain Gerry Morris. Thank you all for your service and friendship over the years.

Brigadier General John Sherman Crow and the entire Blackhorse Association for all of your support during our deployment. I hope we made you proud.

Drill Sergeants Johnson and Dalton, thank you for convincing me that there's nothing to it but to do it and whenever possible not to be a soup sandwich.

Finally, to all those with whom I have served over the last 23 years. You were the foundation of all that went into *Combat Finance*. I owe you more than I can ever repay. I loved serving with you in the military; especially being in a combat arms unit affiliated with the 11th Armored Cavalry Regiment (ACR). No matter what the task or how good we were at that moment, we all wanted to be better, and we worked hard to improve ourselves. We all wanted to be the best troopers we could be, to be in the best tank crew and fire top gun on Table VIII or win the next battle against Blue Force in the central corridor at the National Training Center (NTC) at Fort Irwin, California. Regardless of the situation, our mantra was that we are only as good as our next fight. We also understood that one of the best ways to get better at anything is to learn from our mistakes, but that it was even better to learn from someone else's mistakes. There is no need to walk into an ambush in the Brown and Debnam pass if you have seen others make that mistake before. It seems we all make enough mistakes on our own, so why add to the count with ones we can avoid by being observant? These were powerful life lessons that I feel so fortunate to have been exposed to. We were also fortunate enough to be in a regiment that rewarded drive and initiative. We were always praised more for showing initiative with a bold or daring effort than we were for playing it safe, so long as we did not violate moral, ethical, or known safety guidelines in doing so.

Without the spirit of initiative and constant self-improvement that the Wildhorse Squadron and the Blackhorse Regiment instilled in me, I would not have had the experience necessary to write *Combat Finance*.

Allons!

Introduction

Every day in this country, someone will stop and salute a complete stranger headed home from Afghanistan. Someone will thank a passerby who just finished basic training. Someone will shake a service member's hand on the way to a new assignment. There is a level of honor and respect for people who have served, a respect reinforced by military values, discipline, and self-sacrificing morals. I have had the chance to serve with people who live these values and whom I greatly admire. A few years ago, I was deployed to Afghanistan with the Nevada Army National Guard with a group of disciplined young men and women who, through years of work, were ready to serve their country. It got me thinking: If the military can establish a shared set of leadership and service values and apply them to a process that consistently leads to success, why can't we develop a set of leadership and service values in a process to help individuals and families to consistently achieve financial success? So I embarked on the journey of *Combat Finance* to tell the stories of those who serve our country and how their values, discipline, and morals can teach us financial lessons in our personal lives by using military principles and tactics as a foundation to understand finances in mainstream America.

My motivation to write this book came from Captain Doug Seymour, a witty guy I have worked with in the guard for more than a decade. At the time we served together in Afghanistan I was the executive officer, and Seymour was the intelligence officer. We'd be waiting to give the daily brief to our commander, and we'd always have some time to kill, so everyone would ask me financial questions. One day Seymour said, "Sir, you need to write a book and call it *Combat Finance*." He was onto something. The anecdotes or methods I'd use to describe finances to these guys would be in military terms. If someone was asking about this mutual fund or that stock, I would talk about how they needed to look at it the same way we conduct a combined arms operation in the military: with infantry, armor, and artillery supported by close air and logistics all working together.

I learned all these things through experience. I originally enlisted when I was 19 as a way to help pay for college. I later received my commission as an armor officer in 1994 before I spent time as a platoon leader

Dieterz-Cunningham-Seymour-Lau

I told you Captain Seymour was a big guy. From left to right, Captain Dieters, Lieutenant Colonel Cunningham, Captain Seymour, Major Lau.

and troop commander. I eventually became the squadron commander of the very same unit in which I enlisted back in 1990. I started out my career as a financial advisor in 1996, and by 2001 things were really firing on all cylinders. Of the 247 advisors in my training session in New York City, I was ranked first in the firm nationwide at the five-year mark. In 2001 I had just finished a successful command of Alpha Troop, 221st Cavalry and was preparing to step away from the Nevada Army National Guard to focus on my career as a wealth advisor, and then September 11 happened. It just didn't feel right that my men could go to war without me if I resigned my commission, so my wife and I decided that I would do a full 20 years of service and risk possible mobilization. Since my unit was an Armored Reconnaissance Squadron, working as a round-out to the 11th Armored Cavalry Regiment "Blackhorse," I was sure we would be mobilized right away. But our call did not come until July 2009 when we served a nine-month dual mission as the Battle Space Owners of Laghman Province and provided security force platoons to the 13 United States Provincial Reconstruction Teams in Afghanistan. At the same time, my financial career had taken me far, and I was now a senior vice president and Presidents Club member, managing over $200 million in assets for my clients. I worked very hard to build my business, but I've never been so busy as I was as the executive officer of the 221st Cavalry in Afghanistan.

During my time in Afghanistan, I learned a lot about how quickly things can change, which greatly influenced my financial views. It was a tough year for our soldiers, with over 60 Purple Hearts and 23 improvised explosive device attacks on members of our unit. On one particular mission during the latter part of our deployment, Staff Sergeant Shane Baldwin was on a mission in a particularly dangerous area called the Alishing Valley. Utilizing an unmanned aerial vehicle (UAV), we spotted people digging in an improvised explosive device (IED) ahead of Baldwin's convoy, so we were radioing to let him know what was ahead. Unfortunately, Baldwin and his group did not get the full message in time and they sped up to try to catch these people. They went right into it, and the IED exploded under the vehicle. The crew was banged up, but Baldwin took the brunt of the blow. He ended up having his left leg amputated from just below the knee. When we got back to the states and I took command of the unit, the Command Sergeant Major and I went to see Staff Sergeant Baldwin at Walter Reed National Military Medical

Center in Washington, D.C. Little did I know, he had started to work out with cadets at West Point, and he was already beating most of them on the physical fitness test. Baldwin did eventually get strong enough to get back on active duty. For me, Shane Baldwin is a great reminder that although there is adversity in everyone's lives, it's your attitude and determination that allow you to overcome difficult things and accomplish greatness.

Some people are paralyzed by the idea of starting their journey to financial freedom. Maybe the problem seems really big, and they don't know how to attack it. But how do you ruck march 50 miles? One step at a time. So you've got to create a plan and then break finances down into small steps to get there. Patton was famous for saying that a 90-percent plan aggressively executed today is better than a perfect plan tomorrow. *Combat Finance* is designed to take you step by step through the process of managing your finances, one chapter at a time. So don't sit there and worry, take action at the end of each chapter so that you can be promoted and move on. I've even created a glossary of terms at the end of the text to help guide you through these steps. Refer to it as you go, or if you're feeling lost or confused about a concept. You can also go to CombatFinance.com to ask a question or find a wingman to help you through. Just know that at the end of the day you're going to be better for having taken that 90-percent action than you are waiting for years to come up with a perfect plan that is never going to materialize. The minute you come up with the perfect plan, the markets and life and everything else will have morphed and evolved, and it won't be the perfect plan anymore. So throughout *Combat Finance* I'm going to push you to create a good plan and then aggressively pursue it today. Not tomorrow or next week, but today.

You can't accomplish this mission without knowing why you fight. A lot of people might think *fight* is a bad word. But fighting has brought us a lot of wonderful things. We've fought for freedom and equality. We've fought against tyranny. We've made great changes through the good fight. So what are you willing to fight for? Is it your baby daughter who needs to have a bright future and a college education? Is it so that you never have to see your spouse crying over the bills again? Is it to have the retirement you always dreamed about? Figure out why you fight. Hang on to that. Write it down and post it where you will see it every day to remind you not to ease up in this financial fight. Let it drive you through this journey.

There are two sayings my drill sergeant pounded into my brain during basic training. His first saying was negative, designed to make you feel like a total idiot if you did something wrong. The drill sergeant would look you up and down and ask things like, "Are you going to stand like that? You look like a soup sandwich!" Everyone looked puzzled the first time he said it, but he quickly clarified, "There's a ham sandwich . . . there's a peanut butter and jelly sandwich . . . but there's no soup sandwich. If you pour soup between two slices of bread all you get is a handful of mush! You look like a soup sandwich!" Any time he wanted to say something was messed up, it was soup sandwich. I'll use the same phrase here to describe financial situations that are not up to *Combat Finance* standards. Drill Sergeant was a confident, quick-talking man from Chicago, and if he said you looked like soup sandwich, well, you probably did, and you were going to be doing some pushups or cockroaches, or both. I can't make you do pushups in this book, but I *can* remind you of a drill sergeant who was determined to make me a better soldier when I tell you that something regarding your finances is soup sandwich.

His other saying was far more positive: "There's nothing to it but to do it." There really isn't. After you have this knowledge ingrained in your daily financial life, there's nothing left but to simply apply the principles. Many people are so hesitant to take a financial chance that they won't make any decision at all. If you make a decision and things go south a few days later, you need to continue to stick to the fundamentals because they work, and the bumps in the road are just part of the process, just as it is in the military where you have to put people outside the wire if you want to win the war. Sure, you can stay inside the wire all day so no one gets hurt and you feel better, but that's a false sense of security. In finance, bad things are also going to happen along your way to financial success. It doesn't mean that the process was wrong or the decision was wrong, it's just the fog of war and the randomness of life. But if you will commit to taking action and learning the process and discipline that it takes to win your financial freedom, you will succeed.

We will start with basic training, where you will learn the fundamentals of personal finance, which includes things like getting out of debt, living within your means, and establishing a budget. Just like military basic training, these are mission-critical skills that you must learn in order to succeed. It doesn't matter how smart you are, what school you went to, or who your mom or dad are. If you want to enlist in the military, you have to go through basic training to ensure that those basic skills become a part of who you are. Often, people will have developed some very bad financial habits, but those bad habits are not obvious for a variety of different reasons. Perhaps your parents have stepped in from time to time with financial gifts or assistance to bail you out. Or you have received unexpected bonuses that helped pay off a ballooning credit card balance. These kinds of things can mask an underlying problem, which is a lack of financial self-sufficiency. Basic training will help you put the spotlight on where you stand financially so that you can begin the journey to financial freedom knowing exactly where you currently stand, with the fundamental skills in place to take you where you want to go.

After you have mastered basic training, we'll move on to the purpose and importance of reserves. You will learn why, just as in any military operation, you must always have financial reserves and never deploy them carelessly. Next, we'll talk about how to buy a house that you can truly defend and still win the battle to reach your other financial goals. Then we begin advanced individual training. You may not love it now, but when we're finished, I think you'll "love training" just as much as the Sergeant Major and me. I certainly hope so, because ongoing training is essential to reaching your full lifetime financial potential. However, as important as training is, we cannot forget to think defensively as well. So we'll talk about why you need to defend the home front even while you are out there conducting offensive operations.

Next, in Chapter 6, we transition away from the skills, tasks, and discipline you and your family need to master and begin to build your external team. You'll learn about the value of advice and how to select quality advisors in all areas of your life so that you can continue to master your chosen profession while confidently managing your finances. Like any good manager, you'll need to know how to set priorities and allocate resources, so we'll talk about how to take your financial goals and dreams and turn them into actionable, achievable, and measurable objectives so that everyone on your team can work efficiently to accomplish your mission. Finally, we'll talk about asset allocation and diversification in a way that will leave you understanding it better than you ever have before, and perhaps even embracing it for the first time.

So now that you know where we are heading, that's enough talk. Let's move out smartly and win this fight. I hope you'll join me on a journey through *Combat Finance*, starting with financial basic training.

Christmas 2009
Top Row, Command Sergeant Major Richardson, Lieutenant Colonel Cunningham, Major Neddenriep, Major Lau, Captain Adair. Bottom Row, Major Glynn, Captain Morris, Captain Moore, Captain Minnich

Chapter 1

Basic Training

On the day we arrived for basic training at Fort Benning in rural Georgia, the drill sergeant told us that we would soon learn to maintain our military bearing. We had no idea what that meant at the time, but he told us that we would fully understand the concept by the time we graduated basic training, and that it was the foundation of being a professional soldier. If we didn't understand military bearing by the time we graduated basic training, he said he would have failed us as a drill sergeant. It was his duty to make sure that we would not only understand military bearing, but that we would be proud to possess it.

He was right. I am so proud to now understand that military bearing is a soldier, sailor, airman, or marine's ability to conduct him- or herself on duty and to know that it encompasses his or her level of professionalism when dealing with others and his or her approach to military situations. It has two key components: self-discipline and discipline of others. I see self-discipline as maintaining self-control and being accountable for one's own actions. It's the mark of marines with good military bearing to do their duty even when no one else is watching. Arguing with superiors, ignoring military standards, and permitting rule breaking are not consistent with military bearing. I understand discipline of others as calmly instructing to help rectify mistakes. Airmen with military bearing don't yell at subordinates in anger; instead they identify the deficiency and direct corrective action in a professional manner.

Financial bearing is very similar to military bearing in that it encompasses the same level of discipline when dealing with financial decisions and with how you conduct your approach to managing your money. Like military bearing, financial bearing also has two components. The first, self-discipline, is basically the same. We've all been there: sitting in a shop, debating about whether to buy that new TV, those new shoes, or that brand-new leather couch. Maybe you know you can't afford it, but you justify it because you think you deserve it. That's soup sandwich. The only way to avoid making choices that put your own immediate desires over your long-term well-being is to refer to your financial bearing. You don't need or deserve these things if your bank account says otherwise.

The second component of financial bearing is slightly different from military bearing. Instead of the discipline of others, the second component of financial bearing is the emancipation from others. What that means is that you have the composure and confidence to do what is right for you financially, regardless of the influence of others. I know that we all like to think that we are strong and above the influence of others, but if we are honest with ourselves, that is not entirely true. We all make financial decisions at least in part to conform to social norms. These social norms influence the car we think we need to have, the size and neighborhood of the house we buy, and even the clothes we wear. The influence of others is a powerful force that can be both good and bad, so the mark of a person with good financial bearing is to do what is right financially even when someone else *is* watching.

Figure 1.1 shows a boy we saw out on patrol in the Laghman Province of Afghanistan. You can see he's gotv some kind of cardboard slipper strapped to his feet. The corn that he's carrying probably weighs about as much as he does, and it's thrown over his shoulder with a strap. The point is that we can survive at this level of existence if we have to.

Figure 1.1 Boy with Corn
Copyright © CSM James A. Richardson.

Sure, it's not what we want for ourselves and our kids, but at the same time, even without the new TV, those new shoes, or that leather couch you're still better off economically than 99 percent of the world. So be content with the present while you work to improve the future.

Financial bearing is so important, because in my experience most financial wounds are self-inflicted, or what we might call friendly fire. In other words, our day-to-day choices regarding how we spend our time and money are the determining factor in our financial success or failure. One of the things that most often holds people back from becoming wealthy is that they want to act wealthy while they're young. They want to drive a really nice car that they see their older sibling or parents driving. They want to have that house that took their parents or grandparents 20 years to work into. They take extravagant vacations and have to have the latest fashions. If people are disciplined and stick to the fundamentals of investing, eventually they are going to be able to do those things, but not in the beginning. The military is the same way. Someone might see the way General George Patton acted, and want that kind of success right from the start. Once you become a general officer, you can stand back and look around and focus on the big picture issues and have someone take care of the more mundane things and drive your Humvee for you. But can you imagine going into basic training and trying to act that way? How far would you get? You'd probably get kicked out in the first week. At a minimum you'd be mocked by your drill sergeant. You certainly wouldn't get promoted. So the point is that you have to be a good private or a good lieutenant or cadet before you can be a general. You've got to work your way up and build knowledge and experience. It's the same concept with finances. You've got to start small by demonstrating the financial bearing necessary to live within your means and then use the excess income you generate to invest regularly and build your wealth over time. Sure, there are examples of folks who win the lottery or come up with a brilliant business startup, but for most of us, it's about having the knowledge and discipline to manage our finances in a systematic way. As you proceed through this chapter and complete the key tasks, you'll understand financial bearing, and you'll be proud to possess it. You'll be proud that you owe money to no one, and proud that all you own is yours, earned and paid for.

The Fundamentals of Basic Training

Basic training is designed to take recruits and make them into soldiers, sailors, airmen, and marines. Since no one is born into service, we have to be taught by drill sergeants and mentors through a rigorous, continuous process. For example, army basic training lasts nine full weeks and is divided into three phases of three weeks each. Upon arriving, soldiers get a haircut and are issued uniforms and gear. Soldiers do long road marches, obstacle courses, and hand-to-hand combat, as well as learn the basics of land navigation using maps and a compass. They learn about marksmanship and weapons, and continue with even longer road marches while laden with gear. Eventually trainees begin to gain confidence. They complete more advanced training in weapons, marksmanship, land navigation, rappelling, night infiltration, and other more accelerated skills that will lead to their tests and qualifications for graduation.

Basic training was difficult. They break everyone down to the point that you want to give up. The drill sergeant stood right next to us on the rare occasions when we were allowed to call home. All our mail was opened by the drill sergeant, and if there was anything from a girl we'd get mocked and do pushups. If a mom sent cookies, they'd be thrown in the trash in front of us. You become so run down that all you want is just a little sleep. You'll do anything the drill sergeant orders you to do just to relieve your situation a little. For the first few weeks, everything we did was soup sandwich: the way we put our clothes away, the way we made our beds, the way we ate. The process is there to teach you that you cannot survive on your own and that when you fail to meet the standards or pay attention to detail, you put everyone at risk. You will succeed and fail based on whether the whole platoon succeeds or fails. Over time we realized that if your battle buddy fell behind on a run, you'd better help him. If someone in your squad was behind on a ruck march (a long march with a heavy pack), you dropped back and took his pack so that he could catch up. Then you moved on to help another squad to catch up to the rest, and so on. More importantly, you learned to do the right thing and meet the standards even when no one else was watching, because you knew that failing to do the right thing could cost a life in combat. Everyone started to think that way. If any one person failed, we all failed. If someone failed to meet the standard, we no longer needed the Drill Sergeant to say something because we would correct each other and make sure things were done right. I remember getting my first compliment about four weeks in, and I started to feel like I could do anything by the time I left. You may find yourself experiencing the same process during *Combat Finance* basic training. So don't quit or give up when things get tough. Finish the process, and you'll graduate feeling that you can do anything, too.

Three Phases of Basic Training

In all the branches of the military, leaders use basic training to establish values, discipline, and skills for a shared culture. You'll need similar shared financial values to be deeply instilled in you during *Combat Finance* basic training so that they sustain you during difficult times of temptation or hardship. One of the first things you learn at basic training is your general orders. Every soldier is required to memorize them word for word, a process that is expedited by motivational push-ups, the thinking-man position, dying cockroaches, and low crawls. Every soldier in the platoon learned these orders, or we all paid the price. Because I enlisted as an 11 Bravo, which is the Army Infantry, I'm going to use the Army General Orders and army terms throughout this book. The concepts, however, are universal in all branches of the military and apply to your personal financial battle, regardless of your branch of service, or if you're a civilian.

The Army General Orders are:

1. I will guard everything within the limits of my post and quit my post only when properly relieved.
2. I will obey my special orders and perform all my duties in a military manner.
3. I will report violations of my special orders, emergencies, and anything not covered in my instructions to the commander of the relief.

The *Combat Finance* General Orders are similar:

1. I will work diligently to be the best that I can be in my chosen profession and constantly strive for improvement.
2. I will proudly accept the responsibilities that I have to my family, my community, and my country, and I will perform all my duties in a professional manner.
3. I will maintain my financial bearing by living within my means and purchasing only what I have earned, while consistently investing a portion of my income to improve my future.

Both the Army General Orders and the *Combat Finance* General Orders are critically important, despite how simple they appear on the surface. The first general order says that you are in charge of everything within the limits of your post and you're going to stay in charge until relieved. No passing the buck, no blaming someone else, no gray area. *You* are in charge of completing your mission, and when it comes to your personal finances, the first place to start is by making the most out of your chosen profession. I'm going to show you that you can become financially independent whether you make $20,000 a year or $200,000, but I think we'd both agree that you would rather make $200,000. So start by always bringing your "A" Game to your chosen profession, and constantly strive for improvement.

As I see it, the second general order is about personal responsibility. Be proud of who you are and where you are financially; own it. If you are not currently proud about where you are, that's okay; let's make some changes, but you still need to own it. Your duties to your family aren't a burden; they're a blessing. Your community and country are what you make it, so get involved and make a difference. That's what it means to proudly accept your responsibilities.

Finally, the last general order says that no matter what happens out there, you know to report it to the commander of the relief. You see, there is no way the army or any branch of the military could cover all the crazy things that might go wrong in one sentence, so they basically said, "If anything else happens, call the commander of the relief." When it comes to managing your finances over a lifetime, there are also going to be a lot of crazy things happening that we cannot cover in one book, much less one sentence. However, if I can give you one sentence that will help you get through 99 percent of the issues you will face financially, this would be it: I will maintain my financial bearing by living within my means and purchasing only what I have earned, while consistently investing a portion of my income to improve my future. That is why it is your third *Combat Finance* general order.

I want you to write these general orders down and then memorize them over time. Refer to them when you are faced with financial decisions in your life, and apply them as you complete each of the key tasks in the book. We're about to enter basic training, and your general orders will help you make it through.

No one can force you to go through basic training—military or financial. You have to volunteer. Who would volunteer to go unless you knew it would give you a brighter future? Volunteer and commit now to *Combat Finance* basic training, and I know you can achieve financial victory. Boot camp is where you, a civilian recruit, are transformed into a professional service member to prepare you for eventual deployment into the combat zone. *Combat Finance* basic training will also prepare you to begin your march into financial battle. Basic training will be divided into three phases: (1) live within your means, (2) pay off debt, and (3) nothing to it but to do it.

Phase 1: Live within Your Means

My drill sergeant used to say that you'll be successful in the army as long as you make sure you're in the right place, at the right time, in the right uniform, with the right equipment, and with the right attitude. He was right, and I firmly believe that financial success is the same way.

Believe it or not, living within a set budget is the toughest part for most people. Just like boot camp, this first phase is so hard because it breaks you down to the point where you feel that you can't go on. You thought you were tough until you were given tasks so far beyond your current physical and mental capabilities that you just want to quit. For many people, the first time they really take a hard look at where they are financially can be very similar because they had always convinced themselves that they were financially tough, but the truth is that they had just never been challenged. In this first phase, you must challenge yourself to face the cold hard facts about where you stand financially. If a drill sergeant holds back instead of pushing marines to their limit, he's not helped them; he has only increased the chance that the marines might never come home from a deployment to see their families.

So let's get serious here. You have three key tasks in the first phase.

KEY TASK 1: Ask yourself these questions:

1. What is my monthly gross income?
2. What are my monthly deductions?
3. What is my net take-home income?

Write all these down, and make sure that you're thorough about noting your monthly deductions. To get the correct deductions, go through your paychecks for the past six months and check taxes, social security, medical coverage, life insurance, retirement, and other numbers. Go through it with your human resources representative or your

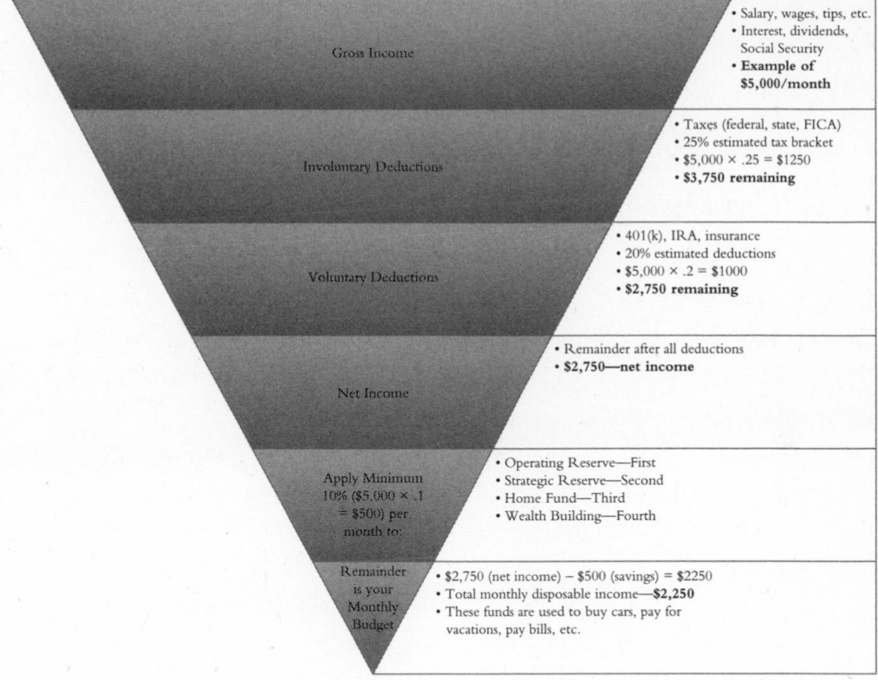

Figure 1.2 How Much Can I Spend?

supervisor to make sure that what you signed up for is correct on your monthly paycheck and in their records. Take a look at Figure 1.2 for an example of why it is so important to accurately identify all your deductions. As you can see, there may be more of them than you originally thought, and they can add up fast. Take the time to make sure your deductions are accurate and that you are not paying for any deductions that you don't need. Your goal here is to ensure that you are paying for all the things that you have to pay for first, so that you know how much of your income is actually available for your remaining wants and needs.

KEY TASK 2: Understand where your money is currently going. To do that, you'll need to ask yourself another three questions:

1. What are my current monthly needs expenses?
2. What do I really *need*, and can I make adjustments to reduce my monthly expenses?
3. Did I check my needs list against the *Combat Finance* budget checklist? (Figure 1.3)

INFLOWS

Salary	$__________
Dividends	$__________
Interest	$__________
Rental Income	$__________
Pension	$__________
Social Security	$__________
Drill/Reserve Pay	$__________
Other	$__________
Total Inflows	$__________

OUTFLOWS

Needs

Mortgage/Rent	$__________
Health insurance	$__________
Prescriptions	$__________
Taxes (divide by 12 if paid annually)	$__________
Utilities	$__________
Groceries	$__________
Child Care	$__________

Non-Essentials

Entertainment	$__________
Auto(s) Replacement Savings Budget*	$__________
Auto Insurance/Fuel/Registration/Maintenance Savings Budget*	$__________
Clothing Replacement Budget*	$__________
Cell Phone	$__________
Personal Care	$__________
Tuition Savings Budget*	$__________
Pet Supplies	$__________
Club Dues (fitness, golf club, Rotary, etc.)	$__________
Travel Savings Budget*	$__________
Gifts Savings Budget*	$__________
Other	$__________
Total Outflows	$__________

Subtract Total Outflows from Total Inflows
to Find Your Total Monthly Surplus or Shortage

Total Net $__________

*A savings budget is an amount set aside to use for a predetermined expense in the future, such as a new car, Christmas gifts, or travel.

Figure 1.3 Budget Checklist

You need to be excessively specific as you develop your monthly needs budget. It doesn't help you to generalize or skip over categories of spending that you could outline here. The budget checklist in Figure 1.3 is a good start, but you can add other categories as needed. A great way to do this is to print out one to six months of bank statements (or corresponding receipts) and categorize them into your budget checklist. I have helped many clients with budgeting over the years, and it always surprises people to see what their actual expenses are versus what they thought they were. One particular client had four daughters, and she was very specific in most of her budget, but I saw one line for personal care listed at only $50 per month. I asked her if she was sure about this, and she said yes, that her family is very frugal with its personal-care budget. Then we looked through six months of her checkbook and totaled up the cost of haircuts, makeup, salon visits, and other personal items, and she was shocked. She had no idea it was so high. Looking at a few months' worth of bank statements will help you be accurate in understanding what you spend. Once you know what you are actually spending, you can look at areas where you might be able to save and reevaluate those areas every few months. You'll find that once you know where your money is going, you'll find many ways to reduce spending with little to no effect on your quality of life or your happiness.

See the Money Saving Tips section of this chapter and log on to CombatFinance.com for more ideas to help you establish your budget.

KEY TASK 3: Take corrective action to ensure that your income from your first key task exceeds your spending from your second key task.

This can be a tough step because you should be looking at the amount you actually spend each month on different needs and wants. The gap might be huge at first, but now you can take steps to close that gap. If you do have a negative gap, the math is easy; you either have to make more money or spend less. Remember, a 40-hour-per-week job is just a start. If you want to close the gap between your income and your spending, one way to do that is to work a second or third job. The reward to get back to a 40-hour work week is when you have all your debts paid off. Think about the photo of the boy carrying corn in Afghanistan. He's working way more than 40 hours a week and still can't afford the nice things you probably have, so keep some perspective on how good we have it in this country. Can you match your work ethic to his? Are you willing to bring the fight needed to get your finances in order?

When it comes to needs, you should think about needing to have a place to live, but that doesn't necessarily mean a nice apartment by yourself where you're not sharing the utilities. Live less expensively with roommates, in your parents' basement, in a cheaper part of town, or in smaller square footage. Perhaps you do need a safe car, but safety and reliability are not justifications for buying a brand new car. You can drive a three- to five-year-old car, and it will be just as safe and under warranty. You do need to eat, but you don't need to eat out. Drink water out of the tap instead of ordering bottled water. Use store brands

Donkey Cart

Tell me again why you need a $50,000 SUV? Build your reserves, your FOB, and your future first. If you can still afford to pay cash for it after that, then go ahead and buy it, but don't tell me you *need* it.

instead of name brands. Think of ways you can close the gap between the expenses and the income. When you do, I know you'll find that many of the ideas you come up with don't negatively affect your quality of life in the slightest.

Money Saving Tips

1. Increase your insurance deductibles on your vehicles and home policies. This is especially true if you have set aside the recommended 6-to 12-months' worth of living expenses for emergency situations.
2. Use one credit card that offers cash-back rewards. This card needs to be paid off at the end of each month.
3. Install motion-activated light switches to decrease your power consumption.
4. Rent more economical cars for short out of town trips, especially during the weekends when rates are as low as $19.99 per day.
5. Pay your mortgage twice a month instead of once a month. By doing so, you will make 26 half payments (52 weeks in a year divided by two). In one year this will equal 13 full monthly payments or one full extra mortgage payment per year.
6. Renegotiate your current credit card rate. This is one of the easiest things you can do to save money, especially if you have a good track record with the company. Simply call and let the representative know that you are shopping rates on cards and would like to know what the lowest available rate is. If they tell you that you already have the lowest rate, politely ask to speak to a supervisor. If you still cannot get a better rate, ask how you can close

(Continued)

Money Saving Tips (*Continued*)

the account. Once you broach this topic, you will be sent to another department responsible for account retention. Their job is to keep you from closing the account. Remember, always be polite, and never lose your cool.

7. If you have multiple balances on credit cards, consolidate your credit card debt to one card with the lowest rate or even a 0 percent rate.
8. If you are a member of a gym and you attend less than twice per week, switch from a monthly flat fee and pay per visit.
9. When traveling and in need of a hotel room, use sites such as Hotwire or apps such as Hotel Tonight to find great rates on unsold, last-minute hotel rooms. Often you can get a rate that is 40 percent lower than the advertised rate.
10. Consider a prepaid phone plan with unlimited texting for younger users if they do not make frequent phone calls.
11. Use sites such as Craigslist and eBay to sell unwanted items and to find bargains on items that you need.
12. Shop your cable provider's rates every year and compare to what new subscribers are being offered from satellite providers. Often cable providers will match a competitor's rate or offer you the new subscriber rate for a certain period of time. Once that period ends, call again and renegotiate.

You Need a Wingman Let's face it, sometimes we all need help staying disciplined enough to break bad habits and stay on course, especially when we're in new, unfamiliar situations. That's why you need a wingman (or, as we call it in the army, a battle buddy). If you've seen *Top Gun,* you know you never leave your wingman, no matter what. You know where your wingman is at all times, and you watch his or her back just like he or she watches yours. So I want you to go through *Combat*

Finance with a wingman. If you are married, then your spouse and your family really need to be your wingmen. If you are single, find a friend to join you on this journey or go to CombatFinance.com to find a wingman. Your wingman, of course, is not your enemy. I see families who see each other as the enemy because maybe there's one member of the family who's a spender and one's a saver, and it creates a constant battle. What if you have two officers or two soldiers or two noncommissioned officers or any two people in the same unit who disagree and they still need to go into battle together? In the military it's understood that there is a chain of command, so the ranking person makes the call, and you move out. In families it doesn't quite work that way. Believe me, I've tried assuming that I was the ranking officer in our family, and it didn't really work out the way I expected, but my wife and I did agree on many financial philosophies and decisions. We had to sit down over a series of weekends and figure out how to balance her desire to live life fully now, with my desire to ensure our future security and success. Once we sat down and really listened to each other to find out not only *what* was important to the other person when it comes to finances, but *why* it was important, we became an unstoppable team, and have been one ever since.

Of course your family's conversations are going to be different from ours, but the underlying principles should be the same. It should boil down to mature discussions about money and what your goals are as a family. Take the time to listen and find out what is important to your spouse and why. I think the lesson for families, spouses, siblings, and other financial partnerships is that, at the end of the day, you've got to come up with a working relationship, even if you disagree on certain details. You have to agree on what the mission is, what the end state looks like, and what your key tasks are. If you fight as a team instead of treating each other as enemies, you will accomplish the mission, and you will reach your financial goals.

"A" Way to Save and Invest One of the instructors at the Armor Officer Basic Course often described examples of how to do things as "A" way. He told us that sometimes the army spells out exactly how something must be done, such as the steps required to clear the main gun of an M1 tank. Other times, the army teaches principles and expects its soldiers, officers, and noncommissioned officers to apply those principles to the current situation and accomplish the mission. In these circumstances, he would preface his examples by saying that it is "A" way, and not necessarily "The" way to do it. I will use this method throughout *Combat Finance* to share experiences that I believe will help you understand the principles at hand, but it is up to you to develop *your* way.

When I enlisted in the National Guard at age 19, I invested each of my paychecks into a brokerage account and never touched them. Since the Guard was my second job and I paid my bills with my "day" job, I was able to do this. When direct deposit became available, I had them go right into my investment account and never strayed from that, even when they would have allowed me a larger house or a fun vacation. Over the next 12 years, my guard paychecks increased, and my investments in the account grew, and that investment account built up to over $100,000. At that level, even a 6 percent annual pretax return would generate, on average, over $500 per month. Some years my investments did better than 6 percent and sometimes worse, but at an average return of just 6 percent, it was more than I was being paid as a company commander for a drill weekend. In a little over 12 years, my money was earning, on average, more than I was. I have continued to invest my guard checks and reinvested all my investment earnings, and the results have been amazing. The point is not to brag, but to demonstrate that what started out as just a few hundred dollars a month and seemed to grow so slowly in the beginning is now a substantial amount of capital that I can use for all kinds of investment opportunities. You can do the same thing, but to get this capital you have to work hard enough and smart enough to invest a portion of what you make to build for your future. The wealth you build is part of your arsenal. How effective can an army be with soldiers but no weapons or equipment? You have to invest to buy those financial weapons and equipment so that you can build an effective financial force over time.

I used many ways to live within my means over the years. Some of the things that I did early in my life weren't necessarily things that I wanted to do, but they paid off. For example, my father had a heart attack during my junior year in high school. He survived, but it wiped him out financially. Even though he was a financial advisor, he didn't have disability insurance. So even though he had life insurance and savings, there was nothing to keep the money coming in while he was out of work for several months. There was just no possibility that he was going to be able to help pay for my college education, so to be able to go to the University of Nevada, I got a cross-country scholarship, and I lived at home my freshman year. Sure, I had dreams of going to Stanford, but that was out of the question because I wanted to stay out of debt. I would have loved to live in the dorms, but I wasn't going to take on student loans. I enlisted in the Army Guard the minute I found out that the cross-country team wasn't working out. When I came home from basic training, I had an enlistment bonus, and I wanted to find a way to move out of my parents' home but still stay out of consumer and education debt. I started looking at the paper for condos and houses for sale. My idea was that if I could get one cheap enough and rent the other room out, I could afford to live on my own.

I knew I couldn't qualify for a real estate loan, and I didn't have a big down payment, so I was looking for situations in which someone could carry the loan. I went to some real estate companies I had done handyman work for, and I asked them if they had anything that was run-down or people wanted to get rid of. A client came in and wanted to get rid of his condo because the tenants had trashed it. He was faced with either putting a lot of money into the condo to get the repairs done and attract a good tenant, or selling it at a discounted price because of the poor condition. Since most lenders would not have approved a loan in the current condition, he carried the mortgage with very little money down. I bought used carpet from a business that was remodeling and went to building supply stores and bought odd-lot and bargain-bin supplies. In just a few weeks I had completely repaired this two-bedroom, one-bath condo. I was out a few bucks; for materials, and I had put in a ton of my own labor. The rent I charged my roommate paid some of the mortgage, and we split the utilities. And, sure enough, it worked. I moved out of my parents' house and enjoyed being on my own. I couldn't afford a car yet, so I rode my bike six miles each way to school and then out to a neighboring community for a construction job, even in the dead of winter. I was in good shape, so I tried to beat my time each day on the bike.

I made it a game. It's not easy to ride a bike in Reno snow, but it worked for me. I did that for a year and half until my boss offered to let me buy one of his old construction trucks for $500. I sanded the company logo off the side and drove around in this truck with bare spots on the side. Of course I wanted a nicer car, but it ran and had a heater, and that's all I really needed.

Along with my construction job, I had a job at a casino working the swing shift in valet. In addition to the minimum wage that they paid, I made $80 to $120 a night in tips. My strategy was to use the paycheck to cover the mortgage and my share of the utilities. Then I would take $50 out of my tips each night and at the end of the week I would put that into my investment account. The remaining $30 to $70 per night in tips was my money for food, groceries, or whatever else I needed. I saved the money from the construction job to pay my tuition that wasn't covered by the G.I. Bill each semester. Although it wasn't the way I'd dreamed of college, it was a way to make my income greater than my expenses, which is also your mission in financial boot camp. If you're in a house bigger than you can afford, think about bringing in roommates or downsizing. If you bought a car that you can't afford, think about downgrading to something more manageable. When you are willing to make those hard choices that get the expenses lower than the income or to raise that income by working a second job or being more successful at the first job, then you will begin to get ahead financially, and you will build wealth. As I said before, the math is simple; you must bring in more than you spend if you want to build wealth.

Phase 2: Pay Off Consumer Debts

Once you have a handle on the first phase of *Combat Finance* basic training, move on to the second phase of paying off consumer debts.

KEY TASK 1: List all the debt you have.

What do you owe on credit cards? On school loans? To family members? Hold back your home loan from this list as we will discuss that in a later chapter.

KEY TASK 2: List the interest rates on each of these debts.

Your interest rate is usually listed on your statement as a percentage under your total due. Some interest rates are higher than others, and others are variable, depending on the type of debt.

KEY TASK 3: Rank all your debts starting from the highest interest rate to the lowest.

Use the Debt Worksheet in Figure 1.4 to rank your debts. If the debt has a balloon payment and is a similar interest rate to another debt, place the one with the balloon payment above the one without the balloon payment.

KEY TASK 4: Calculate your total monthly interest payments on debt.

Take the amount of each debt and multiply it by the interest rate and divide by 12. For example, if you have $8,000 in credit card debt at 17 percent interest, that would be [(8,000 × .17)/12] = $113.33 interest per month. Add the monthly interest for each debt into one total. This is the amount you must budget just to stay even and not incur more debt. See Figure 1.5 to see an example of what this step will look like once you take the debts you ranked in Figure 1.4 and apply the formula to determine your total monthly interest payments.

KEY TASK 5: Calculate a debt payoff plan.

Determine a target date to pay off all your consumer debts. How many months away is that? By the way, if you set a goal that is greater than 24 months, that's soup sandwich. If you need to, go back to Phase I, get your expenses down and set a debt payoff goal that is closer to one year or less, but two years at a *maximum*. Take the total amount of your debts and divide by the number of months to your goal. This is the amount of principal you must pay each month, but you must pay this principal *and* all interest calculated in your fourth key task each month to meet your goal.

List all of your consumer debt starting with the highest interest rate. If a debt has a balloon payment, list that as well along with the due date of the balloon payment.

Creditor	Amount Owed	Rate	Balloon Payment? Y/N	Balloon Payment Due Date

Once you have listed all of your debts, multiply each outstanding balance by the rate and divide by 12.

(Amount Owed × Rate)/12 = Monthly Payment

Amount Owed	Multiply by Rate	Total	Divide by 12	Monthly Payment
			Total Per Month ➡	

Now take each monthly amount and add them together. This is the amount needed to sustain your debt level each month. This does not include additional charges or fees that may hit the account.

Figure 1.4 Debt Worksheet

List all of your consumer debt, starting with the highest interest rate. If a debt has a balloon payment, list that as well along with the due date of the balloon payment.

Creditor	Amount Owed	Rate	Balloon Payment? Y/N	Balloon Payment Due Date
Visa #1	$6,000	21.9%	N	
RV Loan	$36,000	12.4%	Y	7/31/2019
Car Loan # 1	$22,000	5.0%	N	
Car Loan #2	$13,000	4.8%	N	
Student Loan #1	$12,000	4.25%	N	
Student Loan #2	$6,500	4.0%	N	
Visa #2	$8,000	0.09%	N	

Once you have listed all of your debts, multiply each outstanding balance by the rate and divide by 12.

(Amount Owed × Rate)/12 = Monthly Payment

Amount Owed	Multiply by Rate	Total	Divide by 12	Monthly Payment
$6,000	.219	$1314	(1314/12)	$109.50
$36,000	.124	$4464	(4464/12)	$372.00
$22,000	.05	$1100	(1100/12)	$91.67
$13,000	.048	$624	(624/12)	$52.00
$12,000	.0425	$510	(510/12)	$42.50
$6,500	.04	$260	(260/12)	$21.67
$8,000	.009	$72	(72/12)	$6.00
			Total Per Month ➡	**$695.34**

Now take each monthly amount and add them together. This is the amount needed to sustain your debt level each month. This does not include additional charges or fees that may hit the account.

Figure 1.5 Debt Worksheet Example

Consumer debt is unacceptable; it violates everything about financial bearing and our general orders. If we live in a country as rich as the United States and cannot afford something with cash, then we don't get to buy it. Consumer debt can be credit card debt, pay-day loans, store credit, or car loans, and is used for consumption items that go down in value over time. If a year from now you can't sell it for more than you bought it, then it is a consumption item, and you need to pay cash for it out of your monthly budget. And that doesn't mean you get to justify an antique gun purchase with debt just because a TV show says it's going to be worth a bunch more. Remember, whether it's an issue of discipline or feeling like you have to impress others, your financial bearing and general orders can help you be smarter about getting rid of debt.

There's this derogatory term in the military called the PX Ranger. The PX is the Post Exchange where people can buy all sorts of products on base, including awards and medals. PX Rangers are soldiers who want to look as though they've won an award or received a promotion that wasn't earned, so they go to the exchange and buy all sorts of stuff and put it on their uniform. All military personnel who live the values of their branch of service understand that those purchased items do not make a great warrior. True respect cannot be bought; it must be earned. In a similar way, a lot of people use debts to appear wealthy, thinking that they can buy respect. They'll have a fancy car and pretend that they're doing financially well, but if many of them lost their jobs, they would have to give up their items within 30 days because it's all a façade with no foundation. You can have all the medals in the world, but if none of it is earned, then it means nothing. Likewise, you can have all the fancy clothes and leased cars you can get your hands on, but it will not lead you to true wealth or financial independence. Instead, if you truly want to become wealthy and not just fake it, then it's time to buckle down, stop making excuses, and get your numbers in order. As our drill sergeants taught us, the maximum effective range of an excuse is zero meters, so let's get going and attack any debts you have.

Part of the value of boot camp is learning the importance of uniformity and the discipline of understanding that, at first, things might seem a little dumbed down. But what you eventually find out is that what you're doing is creating a system and a process, something that is both consistent and repeatable. By establishing uniformity, everyone, including you, knows what to expect, and, therefore, you don't have to rethink the small, minute things in times of stress. You can focus on the big things that lead to success as a unit. There is truly a lot of freedom in that, both in a military sense and in a financial sense. In times of chaos, everyone knows where to grab that first-aid kit because it's always in the left pocket of a specific soldier. Everyone knows that if you have to jump over to another vehicle, the ammo cans are in the same place. Everyone knows what is normal and what is expected. Eventually, that leads to efficiency and a certain pride in upholding these standards because deterioration of those standards can hurt you in the long run. Paying off debt is also about uniformity and financial efficiency, because once you pay it off, you have all of that monthly income freed up to both live better now *and* invest for your future. Phase II is about understanding exactly what your debt is and exactly how you're going to pay it off each month. Take solace and pride in this uniformity and fight for your financial freedom.

Phase 3: Nothing to It but to Do It

There is only one key task in accomplishing your third phase of basic training.

KEY TASK 1: You must ensure that you currently have the income to meet your goal.

Take your needs budget from Phase I and add it to your monthly debt pay-off budget from Phase II. If your needs budget plus debt pay-off budget exceeds your net income, you must either increase your income by working harder, smarter, or more efficiently, by getting a raise at your current job, or by adding a job. You can also decrease your needs budget by finding ways to live that don't require as much capital. This is the most difficult part of your *Combat Finance* basic training. It will pit your desires against your need for financial freedom. Don't let thoughts of living well in the short term get in the way of living well in the long term.

When I think of this last step, I think of a time shortly after I joined the guard when I wore cadet rank. I was still going to drill through what we call a simultaneous-membership program. It's a program in which you're an ROTC cadet, yet you still hold your enlisted position in the unit. They usually put you in with another officer that mentors you, and you get to be the acting platoon leader at times. We were short of lieutenants at the time, so I got thrown in as the acting third platoon leader. So I was a cadet, I was acting as a lieutenant, I was a third platoon leader, but at the same time I was a college student, and I wanted to have fun. I wanted the lack of responsibility that you have while you're going to college. I was even letting my hair grow out a little bit. Who wanted to have a stodgy military haircut when you're on campus? I was tucking it under my hat during drill.

At that time we still went in to get our pay in cash from the captain. "Cadet Neddenriep reporting for pay," I saluted. He saluted back and handed me my pay. And I remember he looked up and cocked his head to the right and said, "And get a goddamn lieutenant's haircut." Just as blunt as that. And I was kind of taken aback, but I said, "Yes, sir," and saluted and walked out. At first, I was pissed, because when someone tells you something you don't want to hear, your first reaction is, "Well, what does he know?" But as I thought more about it, and as I have often thought about it over the 20-some years since then, that was a great moment for me because I realized that it didn't matter what I wanted. Sure, I might have wanted to be the carefree college student. I remember distinctly that I missed a big football game that year because of drill weekend, and all my friends were going to that game because that night U2 was playing in the same town and everybody was going to go to the game and then to the U2 concert. I was so ticked that I had to miss that and go to drill. However, the reality is that I had a responsibility. It didn't matter that I wanted to be a free-spirited college student. I was the acting third platoon leader. Those men deserved to have a platoon leader who was professional, who had his head in the game, who was focused, and who set the right example. The message is that we all have responsibilities that we want to avoid. You have a responsibility, not only to yourself, but as a husband, as a wife, as a father, as a mother, to take control of your money and practice the principles that we talk about in *Combat Finance*. That is what is going to be the best for you and your family in the long run. That's what's going to build the wealth to allow you to take those nice vacations later on, to have that safe and comfortable car later on, to provide a solid college education for your children, to pay for a wedding, and all the other things you dream of.

Basic Training Is Not for Quitters

When people have hit a financial rock bottom, they may be feeling as though they're mired in a state of mediocrity. But you always have the ability to change your fate, and the only way to do that is to develop a careful plan and follow the steps to accomplish it. If you are reading this book, then at some level, you want to change. What made you want to change? You need to reach down, look inside, figure out what it was that caused you to pick up this book, and that's the thing you need to remember every time you feel as though you're about to violate *Combat Finance* principles. This is what you are willing to fight for. Write your reason on a note and put it in your wallet, write it on your mirror, post it on your fridge, and plaster it on your cubicle. Whatever it is, keep that with you at all times and use it to stay on track.

Go analyze your budget and do the math until you have an income greater than your spending, and then review it until you can't get it wrong. Review your reasons for pursuing financial freedom until you can't forget them. Run battle drills for spending restraint scenarios until you just can't help but do the right thing. Get your standard operating procedure for spending down pat. You want to have such a solid plan for this that you don't have to wake up at night worrying about what's going to happen in your financial life. You'll sleep well knowing your mission and that you're going to accomplish it.

In the first few weeks of basic training, whenever I heard the drill sergeant say "soup sandwich," I felt that he was really putting me down, and I was insulted. But by graduation I realized what he was really saying was, "You're better than that." I never said it to you then, but thank you, drill sergeant, for convincing me that there's nothin' to it but to do it.

After Action Review

If you have finished this chapter successfully and have completed the following tasks, you are hereby promoted to Private First Class (PFC) in *Combat Finance*. You have:

- Consistently followed your *Combat Finance* general orders.
- Consistently maintained your financial bearing.
- Developed your monthly budget.
- Inventoried your total debts.
- Completed your consumer debt pay-off plan.

If you have not completed each of the key tasks in this chapter, *continue reading,* but you are barred from promotion until you meet these minimum standards.

Chapter 2

The Purpose and Importance of Reserves

In both my financial advisory practice and in my military career, I am experienced enough to understand that bad things are going to happen from time to time. Although all of us can learn from our mistakes and perhaps avoid similar ones, it is naive to think that new and unique challenges aren't going to confront us in the future. We can see a similar pattern in the wars in Iraq and Afghanistan. In both conflicts, the enemy discovered quickly that direct confrontation with U.S. forces did not turn out well for them, so they adapted to using improvised explosive device (IED) attacks. As we countered with more resistant vehicles, they again adapted to other tactics such as infiltration of the Afghan security forces to attack us from within. The point is that it is folly in both investing and in warfare to think that you can permanently prevent bad things from happening or prevent the situation from evolving.

Therefore, we must maintain constant diligence to succeed financially and on the battlefield.

Most of the time, for instance, our troops aren't under hostile fire in Afghanistan, but if they don't stay diligent about how they will react in those negative situations, then it can turn deadly. If they don't know exactly where their weapons are on their body, that they have been inspected and maintained repeatedly over time, and that they have practiced how to draw and fire under highly stressful circumstances, then they face greater risk on that one day when something does go wrong. In the military, we are constantly training for that one moment. In Afghanistan, there was one section on the way off the Forward Operating Base (FOB) where we had to stop and complete a whole list of safety checks. The sign outlined everything that had to be checked and double-checked. Is your load plan correct? Is everybody strapped in? Is everyone wearing the proper gear? The vehicle commander had to radio in to the Tactical Operations Command (TOC) and say, "I verify our load plan. I verify each one of my crew for proper personal protective equipment and safety restraint gear. We have completed our weapons checks." By stating those things over the radio, he was going on record saying that he had done everything he could to prepare for his patrol outside the wire. He couldn't just give a quick hand wave to dismiss the procedure; it had to be a conscious effort to secure his troops. Just beyond the safety and weapons check was the interior gate, and above it was another, huge sign that read, COMPLACENCY KILLS. We drove by it every time we left the FOB, and it towered over us as a reminder of what happens in theatre when you forget to be diligent about the procedures that seem small or inconsequential.

When we fail to be financially diligent, we also risk huge losses. You've started out your *Combat Finance* journey by living within your means, saving, and making a plan to pay off debt, but there are many situations that can derail you after basic training. Living within your means isn't just about cutting expenses; it's also about developing a safety net for you and your family so that life's seemingly unexpected events don't derail your progress toward financial freedom.

Military and Financial Reserves

The key to preparing a safety net is to develop a series of financial reserves: stockpiles of funds set aside for emergencies or unassigned to immediate tasks so that they can be used as reinforcements or to exploit success. The concept of a financial reserve actually comes from the concept of a military reserve, which is a unit of soldiers not committed to a specific assignment, battle, or mission. These troops are set aside by their commander to be available for unforeseen circumstances and sudden opportunities, and they're preorganized to be on call for defense or to relieve troops who have been fighting for a long time. Reserves come in many shapes, sizes, and forms, from a platoon that might keep back a squad as a reserve, to a company that might keep back a platoon. Every unit will always keep a reserve that is proportionate to its size and configured for its specific mission.

A military reserve is deployed by a commander through a careful, detailed process. Even in tough situations that trigger the use of reserves, a commander will only deploy a portion of them if that will be sufficient to stop an attack or accomplish the mission. Some of the reserve is usually held back to deal with any counterattack that may come after the initial push, or to cover a withdrawal if necessary. The only time that a full reserve is committed is in an extreme crisis where the survival of the entire force is in jeopardy and all hands are needed to prevent being overrun.

Financial reserves are similar. You always need to maintain a backup pool of funds in low-risk liquid investments for when bad things happen to you: loss of a job, sickness, a car accident, a late-in-life career change, or even if you want to take advantage of dips in the market. Different types of reserves can assist you in overcoming or accomplishing each of those tasks. Reserves help you fight those events head-on, allowing you time to search for a new job, get better, fix your car, or pay for things that seem unexpected in life. We address three different types of reserves in this chapter: operational, strategic, and tactical.

Operational Reserve

There will always be times when you need to draw from an immediate reserve that can assist you with small, short-term emergencies that happen in the day-to-day operations of your life. Your operational reserve is a one-month stockpile that you develop in an accelerated amount of time as a stopgap to help ensure your immediate financial well-being in emergency situations. We'll begin your key tasks by building an immediate reserve using the budget you created in chapter one.

KEY TASK 1: Build an operational reserve equal to one month of your needs budget, which you calculated in the first chapter.

- This must be done immediately, first, before debt pay-offs, before contributions to a 401(k), and before contributing to any other financial endeavor.
- There are no simultaneous operations or "wants" expenditures until you build this reserve.
- This account should take no more than three months to establish. If it does?—that's soup sandwich.

You can either choose to build this in a checking account by keeping a minimum balance or by opening a savings account and contributing immediately. Since you cut your expenses in *Combat Finance* basic training, a weekly or monthly contribution to build your operational reserve should not be a problem. The first purpose of your operational reserve is to provide immediate emergency relief for things like short-term auto repair or a roof leak or if your child suddenly needs medical care. For example, if John decided during *Combat Finance* basic training that he needed $4,500 each month to get by on his needs budget, then he would need a $4,500 minimum balance in his checking account at all times or a $4,500 balance in a savings account as his operational reserve. To build that within three months, he needs to make a $1,500 deposit each month until it's established.

The second purpose of your operational reserve is to train you to have money available that you don't spend under any circumstances except true emergencies. It's a lesson in self-restraint, in control, and in determination. In short, it's a way to maintain your financial bearing. One reason that many Americans have difficulty maintaining a reserve is that they convince themselves that they have an emergency every month. Think, instead, that this fund is purely for times when something is on fire, your car is in pieces, or there are six inches of water in your house, and you have no other way to financially deal with the problem. It's not for a new work outfit or a new washing machine or a new computer. Be honest with yourself about what a financial emergency really is: something that threatens your basic abilities to eat, have a roof over your head, or get to work. This reserve is intended as a shock absorber. Many times, we'll face dips and potholes in life, and this fund allows us to absorb those bumps and move on. It prevents raiding your 401(k) or using credit cards to deal with a problem. Any drop below your operational reserve minimum, and you need to replace it immediately. That means cutting your wants down to nothing until it's built back up: no eating out, no vacations, and no new outfits until that fund is back to a full month. Think about creative ways you might initially build this, especially since it needs to happen quickly. Do you have a mountain bike you never use? A collection of designer purses stuffed in the closet? An extra set of golf clubs? Think about selling these items. Your financial security, and building your reserve, are much more important.

Strategic Reserve

In *Combat Finance* we will also build a strategic reserve to be used only in extreme, long-term emergencies such as major accidents, a cancer diagnosis, or a life-changing career switch. This strategic reserve is a mightier reserve than its operational cousin, used for fighting bigger battles and preventing a complete personal financial meltdown. The strategic reserve is 6–24 months' worth of your needs budget in a very safe savings account, money market, or CD account.

I ran into a gentleman years ago who could have really used a strategic reserve. We knew each other because we'd both served in cavalry units and it was clear, while speaking with him, that he had been badly injured. He explained that he'd had an accident while working with machinery, and after multitudes of surgeries, he couldn't work as he once did. He was going through a disability that would forever change his earning potential in his trained profession. He needed to retrain completely to do something else with his career. This is a perfect example of where a strategic reserve comes in. When you're in a situation in which an injury or job loss forces you to blow through your operational reserve, then you need that strategic reserve to help get you to a point where you can work again. And since we never squander reserves, when we are forced to draw from them, we must immediately cut all unnecessary expenditures to make our reserves last as long as possible and to make it easier to rebuild them when we get through the crisis. For example, six months' worth of strategic reserves could last you well over a year if you immediately cut expenses while pursuing other forms of income such as disability or part-time work. If deployed properly and used sparingly, your strategic reserve will keep you from devastating your 401(k) or your kids' college savings plans in times of crisis. General George Patton once said that he didn't like to ever pull back his troops to re-consolidate. Why? He said that he didn't like to pay for the same real estate twice. You worked hard to build those longer-term investment accounts, so don't pay for them twice by failing to build, maintain, and sparingly use your strategic reserve.

KEY TASK 2: Determine the number of months you'll need for a strategic reserve.

A strategic reserve is 6- to 24-months of needs budget, but how do you choose your necessary number of months in this financial stockpile? If you have extreme longevity in your job and you feel that you have almost no risk of losing your employment, your minimum strategic reserve is six months' worth of your needs budget. An example of a person in this category would be someone who has worked for the federal government for more than a decade, and has continually received a raise each year, and is in a position that has little to no risk of elimination. Remember, the needs budget is different from your full budget: it contains only the items you absolutely need to get by, such as basic food, shelter, and transportation to get to work.

For those people who are either self-employed, are working at a new job, work in a volatile industry, or have a company that might be vulnerable, a full year of needs expenses will be required for your strategic reserve. An example of someone in this category would be a construction contractor in a vulnerable market who deals with the ebbs and flows of building and seasonal work. If you are retired or close to retirement and a significant portion of your income comes from investments such as an IRA or 401(k) (as opposed to a dependable pension), then 12- to 24-months of your needs budget is required in your strategic reserve. This will allow you to ride out the storm during difficult markets so that you are not forced to sell investments at a bad time. Remember, if you are retired, the ability to rebuild these investments may not exist, so you must take extra precautions to ensure that you protect them. A 12- to 24-month strategic reserve will help you do that. Use Figure 2.1 to help you determine the strategic reserve level that is appropriate for you and your family. Find the descriptions on the right hand side of Figure 2.1 that best match your situation and then set a strategic reserve target that is within the number of months noted on the left.

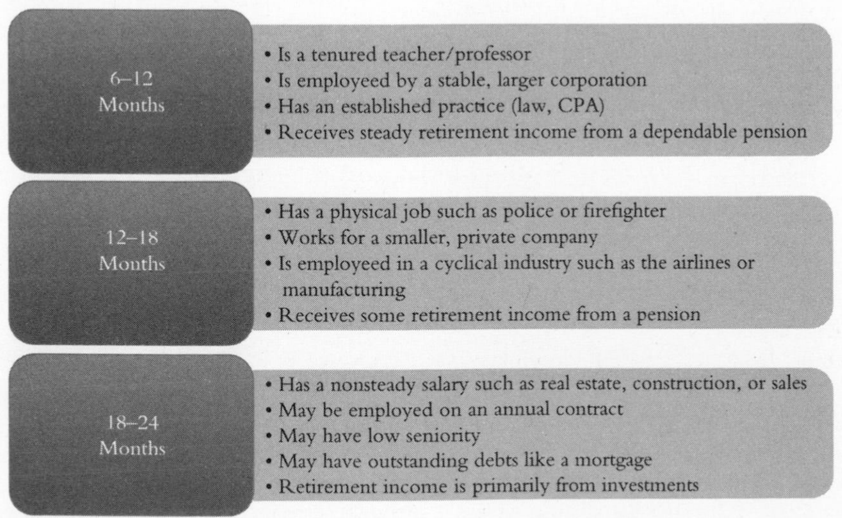

Figure 2.1 Strategic Reserve Guidelines

Monthly Needs

Mortgage/Rent	$________
Health insurance	$________
Prescriptions	$________
Taxes (divide by 12 if paid annually)	$________
Utilities	$________
Groceries	$________
Child Care	$________
Total Monthly Needs Budget	$________

Multiply your total monthly needs budget by the number of months you determined in key task 2.

Total Monthly Needs Budget × 6 to 24 = Strategic Reserves

Refer to the Budget Checklist (Figure 1.3) in Chapter 1 to determine your monthly needs. Then refer to the Strategic Reserves Guidelines (Figure 2.1) in Chapter 2 to determine your level of reserves. If your job is one with a steady salary and has stability like a teacher or police officer, strive for the six-month figure. If your job is volatile and your salary fluctuates like that of a salesman or waitress, set aside 12 months worth of expenses.

Figure 2.2 Strategic Reserves Worksheet (6- to 24-months' worth of needs budget)

KEY TASK 3: Calculate your total strategic reserve amount.

To do this, use the worksheet in Figure 2.2 to multiply your monthly needs budget (from Chapter 1) by the number of months you calculated in your second key task. For example, if George has a $2,400 needs budget for his family and they are business owners in a cyclical industry, they need 12 months' worth of needs expenses in reserve. Their minimum strategic reserve would be $2,400 multiplied by 12: $28,800.

KEY TASK 4: Determine how much you will need to save each month to reach that goal.

To find that, simply divide your strategic reserve goal by the number of months you will need to reach it (no more than 24 months). So if you're George the contractor, you would divide $28,800 by 24 months if you needed the full two years to build it. George would need to stash away $1,200 per month for 24 months to reach his strategic reserve goal after developing his operational reserve. After the operational reserve is built, it's okay to build the strategic reserve over time, but take no more than two years to accomplish that. Taking too long to ensure your family's financial safety is soup sandwich.

You can put this strategic reserve in a savings, money market, or certificate of deposit account, but it must be secure, conservative, and easily accessible. If your strategic reserve minimum is a large number, say $40,000, obviously you're going to want to get more return on that amount than a basic savings account. One solution is to put this money in a laddered CD maturity of three, six, nine, and 12 months as shown in Figure 2.3. If the three-month CD comes due and there has been no emergency, then you would purchase a 12-month CD to replace it, since the original 6-, 9-, and 12-month CDs now are only 3, 6, and 9 months out. If you repeat this process each time a CD comes due, you will end up with a 12-month CD due every 3 months. This system allows you to have access to liquid cash every 90 days yet still benefit from the higher pretax return normally associated with 12-month CDs.

Example of a $40,000 Strategic Reserve Ladder
$10,000 into four CDs, each maturing three months apart.

- CD # 1—$10,000 into a CD that matures in three months.
- CD # 2—$10,000 into a CD that matures in six months.
- CD # 3—$10,000 into a CD that matures in nine months.
- CD # 4—$10,000 into a CD that matures in 12 months.

As CD #1 matures, a 12-month CD would be purchased to replace it, if no emergency is present. When CD #2 matures, it will be replaced with a 12-month CD as well. And so on for CDs #3 and #4. By doing so, you will have funds available every 90 days while at the same time receiving the higher interest rates generally available on one year CDs.

Figure 2.3 CD Ladder Strategy

No unit in the military operates without a reserve. Whether it's a platoon, a company, or even a division, every one of those will have a reserve commensurate to the size of that organization to either shore up a weakness or exploit success. The same principle applies to our individual finances. If you're a college student, your operational reserve might only be $800 in a savings account, but it's there for emergencies. As your career, your finances, and your family grow, the reserves obviously have to be larger. But since we have established that no unit operates without a reserve, don't think that there is any point in your life when you can safely get by without an operational reserve to get you through these all-too-common events. Strategic reserves, on the other hand, are there for the once-in-a-lifetime category of events. They are there to help overcome these extreme issues without derailing all of your other goals and plans in life.

Managing Your Reserves

Remember that both operational and strategic reserves are for use in times of true emergencies only, so if you dip into these reserves, you are on absolute lockdown. No extra expenses will be tolerated while you use and then rebuild your operational and strategic reserves. You must treat the situation as a crisis mode, when you are under attack, and all battle stations are manned. If you understand the value of your reserves and treat them as seriously as I am suggesting, then you will also learn to use as many early warning systems as possible to take actions to protect yourself. For example, when we were in theatre and our intelligence sources indicated that there was an imminent threat, we were much more vigilant about our activities. Instead of just carrying my sidearm on the FOB, I would have my M4 with me at all times. We would place more guards in the watchtowers and increase the number of quick reaction forces that were on call. And what this means in terms of your financial bearing is that if you hear your company may be experiencing layoffs soon, you go into an increased readiness posture. You buckle down on your expenses, you build up extra strategic reserves, and you get yourself ready to fight a financial battle. Once you're under attack—maybe you lost your job—then you increase your posture further, putting all your resources and efforts toward making your strategic reserve last as long as possible while you are fighting your way back to normal.

A good way to prepare for this is to establish standard operating procedures (SOPs), load plans, and battle drills well before you have to face a problem. An SOP is a way to achieve efficiency by doing certain tasks the same way every time, conducting a vehicle search in the most thorough and efficient way possible, for example. A load plan is a way to save time and energy by reducing clutter and chaos, putting the first-aid kit in exactly the same place every time in every Humvee, for example, so that, in an emergency, you know where to find it. Battle drills allow for rapid execution of complex actions. So, for instance, we have an IED battle drill because we commonly face these in theatre. We rehearse who is the primary and alternate for security, for providing aid, and for calling in medevac, and gunners try to pinpoint the triggerman of the IED in their sector of responsibility. We do this because it helps to take the chaos and emotion out of the situation and assists us in reacting swiftly and efficiently to get through the problem. We develop these SOPs using experience and experimentation to see what works, and a great unit will regularly assess and refine their SOPs, load plans, and battle drills over time to make them better.

An investor must also create SOPs, load plans, and battle drills to deal with things like emergency expenses, job loss, market turmoil, and to also exploit targets of opportunity that present themselves. You should discuss commonly encountered financial situations with your family: a layoff, a medical emergency, a career change. Then prepare yourself and your family for that situation as acutely as possible by discussing and prioritizing expenses ahead of time and reaching an understanding of how you would use your strategic reserve sparingly. By discussing these financial matters as a family without the stress of the event, you will be better prepared to make rational choices when a real emergency strikes. If your company conducts layoffs next month, then you go home and alert your family. Since you and your family have already practiced your financial battle drill for this situation, they know that they'll have to cut expenses for things like your child's karate lessons or for clothing purchases or for eating out at restaurants or for cable TV. Planning takes the emotion out of these challenges because you know what you have to do and that it's for a finite amount of time. It makes your response quicker and more efficient. Everyone knows his or her role under stress so it makes it easy to execute. I have had some people tell me that they would never do this because they would not want their spouse and kids to worry that something like this was ever going to happen. Although I respect that concern, I have seen this happen to families in my practice. In every case where it turned out badly, and the relationship did not survive the downturn, the trouble was due to a spouse feeling betrayed. One client told me, "If I had known it was that bad I could have gotten a job at Starbucks, and we didn't have to go on that vacation." Believe me, bad news is not fine wine; it does not get better with age. A family that is open and honest about their finances and sets their priorities and budgets together is much more likely to weather the financial storms that will surely come.

Battle drills aren't always for negative actions. Maybe you built up a reserve that is overflowing. If you've communicated your battle drill to your real estate agent or broker—letting her know that if she sees a great rental property for under $200,000—she will contact you when she sees it, and you'll be able to take advantage of that overflow. Or maybe you have a financial advisor who knows that any time you have more than $25,000 in cash in your account that you would like him to be looking at great bonds or stocks that might meet your needs. Neither of these professionals would be proactive in contacting you about these opportunities if they didn't know your exact battle drills and SOPs for dealing with these positive opportunities. They don't even have to ask; they just know to call you when the opportunity arises because they've been made a part of your SOP.

Load plans can be especially beneficial. For instance, if you have a plan for the way you prepare your receipts and materials for your taxes, then your CPA can be more efficient in the way she prepares your finances for your tax return to be filed with the IRS. Or maybe you give your attorney exact copies of all your supporting beneficiary information for your 401(k). That type of load plan allows your attorney to verify and support any claims you or your family might have in the case of beneficiary issues. Battle drills, SOPs, and load plans reduce friction by reducing chaos and confusion and focusing energy and efforts toward making the operation as smooth as possible.

Simultaneous Operations

Now, unlike your operational reserve, which you must build before any other financial endeavor, you may conduct simultaneous operations while you build your strategic reserve. While you are saving for your strategic reserve minimum, you are probably also paying down debt, or saving for a house, or funding your 401(k). These can all be done simultaneously, but remember, your operational and strategic reserves are completely separate funds and should not be commingled with savings for a house or new car. In Afghanistan we were working to sustain security for elections, but we were also doing IED patrols and other operations in support of the Afghan government at the same time. We had multiple lines of effort. It is important to build a strategic reserve, but you don't need to stop doing everything else. With the hard work, savings, and cuts you've made to your monthly budget in basic training, these items shouldn't be difficult to do at the same time. Keep in mind, though, that it is okay to only do minimum payments on your student loans and other long-term debt until you establish your operational and strategic reserves completely. I do recommend that you contribute enough to get a full match on any 401(k) if your company offers it because it's free money. You can increase your contributions to your 401(k) beyond the company's matching level later, after both your operational and strategic reserves are established, but just make sure you're contributing enough that you get a full employer match until then.

Building a strategic reserve that allows you to overcome a large change or problem at some point in your lifetime will give you the freedom to work through it and continue on to a brighter financial future, rather than watching years of work deteriorate because of one event. Sun Tzu says that every battle is won or lost before it's even fought, and you can use that to describe why people need to have a strategic reserve. Some people will argue that holding back such sizable reserves is a mistake, because they could invest that money and get a better return. It's true; you could make a lot of money on some opportunities that come along. So many people will justify the use of their strategic reserve money in this way because they truly believe that some life events are "unexpected," and they feel that this hefty reserve is just sitting there being unused. They believe that car accidents and cancer and job loss only happen to people who are unlucky. The problem is, statistically, these things happen to people all the time. Chances are that you will face some "unexpected" challenge at some point in your life. But I have seen it over and over again. The moment you give up your reserve is when trouble strikes. You get in an auto accident at the same time that you decided to buy into a non-liquid commercial building project with your strategic reserves because you felt like bad things could never happen to you. But now you need the cash that a strategic reserve provides and, lo and behold, the markets are down, your 401(k) is down, and everyone who could normally help you is short on cash. So now you're digging yourself out of a financial hole in a very expensive and long-term way. Just like Sun Tzu said, that battle was lost the minute those strategic reserves were depleted and you were walking around exposed, not months later when the emergency actually hit.

A strategic reserve isn't just "sitting there," it's a financial strategy to sustain you during your darkest times. Its purpose is to wait in a holding pattern until it is most needed, and at that point, if you are diligent about having it available, it will help you shine in a moment when everything else is in the johnny. Did you know that hundreds of years ago sea captains were taught to pace the deck with their hands clasped behind their backs, under the coattail? This was so that in the heat of battle the pacing would keep their legs and voice from shaking, and the coattail would hide any tremble of the hands or whiteness of the knuckles. Your strategic reserve will allow you to be the steady, level-headed, commanding presence in the heat of battle. If you keep your financial bearing, you will have plenty of opportunity to invest over your lifetime. I want you to take advantage of the good ones when they come along, but never with your operational or strategic reserves.

Tactical Reserves

The final type of reserve I want you to keep are tactical reserves. Tactical reserves are kept in every type of investment account you create over time. For example, I want you to have a small tactical reserve in your 401(k) to use for buying on dips in the market. I want you to maintain a tactical reserve in your stock, bond, and real estate wealth-building accounts so that you are ready to strike when the time is right. These reserves are different from your operational and strategic reserves in that it is perfectly acceptable to deplete them from time to time to take advantage of opportunity. Let's look at an example. Hank may have a 401(k) that has a well-diversified asset allocation: fixed income, domestic and foreign stocks, real estate investment trusts, and maybe even a little bit of his own company's stock. Each of these assets has different capabilities, limitations, and risk levels, so over time Hank will be best served by staying diversified in all of them. But what if Hank had a 5 percent tactical reserve in his 401(k) when the stock market lost over 50 percent of its value from late 2007 through early 2009? With such a dramatic sell-off, Hank may decide to use his 5 percent 401(k) tactical reserve to buy into one of the U.S. stock mutual funds available in his 401(k) plan. Of course, a well-diversified portfolio is the best way to invest your 401(k) over the long run, but there is nothing wrong with having a small tactical reserve ready to take advantage of extreme conditions when they come along. Yes, that tactical reserve in the 401(k) is only earning a cash interest rate while you wait, and it's not much, but its ability to help build wealth by deploying it at the right time makes it far more valuable than its simple interest rate. Now, in this example it worked well for Hank: The S&P 500 has almost doubled since hitting a low in early 2009. But what if that didn't happen? Well, Hank's 401(k) is a long-term investment, and he continued to make his monthly contributions and stay well-diversified even after deploying the tactical reserve, so he would still be in great shape. Remember, he did not risk his operational or strategic reserve; he simply deployed one of his tactical reserves in a manner consistent with his investment objective for the 401(k).

Hank might also have a tactical reserve built into an investment account like a municipal bond account. He could hold out a 5 percent cash reserve in that account that would allow him to buy into a new high quality bond that he spots. At that point, he would've completely depleted his tactical reserve in that account, but he could allow that reserve to build back up through the interest paid by the bonds or through his own regular contributions. After the tactical reserve is built again, he could go out and grab more new bonds with that reserve. Success happens when preparation meets opportunity. Your tactical reserves prepare you for that introduction.

There are several reasons why you need a tactical reserve for each of these missions, but the primary one is that it can be difficult to move money between these separate accounts. You can't take your 401(k) tactical reserve and move it to your daughter's college savings 529 plan account without serious tax consequences. You can't take real estate tactical reserve and write a check into your 401(k), because it has to come from payroll deductions. So if you want to be ready to strike when the time is right, you must create tactical reserves throughout the spectrum of investments that you build over time.

It's important to note that, in these accounts—401(k) and wealth building—you should maintain your overall target allocation and never dip into the principal of the investment. The reserve is there to allow you to freely maneuver during times of market stress, and you can always use dividends, interest, or realized capital gains from these investments to rebuild your reserve, but you never touch the principal. If you allow it to accumulate over time, that accumulation can eventually provide cash flow that can last a lifetime. Sometimes, the cash flow that this accumulation provides becomes larger than the amount you earn from your labor (your employment). I call that financial independence: when your money consistently makes more each year than you do through your employment.

Remember Your Reserves

Operational Reserve—One month's worth of needs budget.
Strategic Reserve—6- to 24-months' worth of needs budget.
Tactical Reserve—Kept inside every type of investment account, used to buy during dips in the market.

A Final Note about Reserves

When I begin a new client relationship, I often encounter some initial resistance to creating such strong reserves. Some clients will ask, "Why should I save and save and save and never enjoy my life? Isn't the whole purpose of making money so that I can enjoy it before I die?" My answer to that is that building your reserves is a lot like basic training in that the strength, resilience, and confidence that both provide will last you a lifetime if you are willing to sacrifice for a relatively short time to get the job done. Now, at 42 years of age I would not want to go back to basic training if I didn't have to, but I'm glad I went through it once because I have benefited so much in the past 23 years from the lessons the drill sergeant taught me. I also wouldn't want to be forced to rebuild my reserves from scratch, which is why I do not use them lightly. But if you commit to building your reserves now and working your way through *Combat Finance*, I know that you will have the best chance to enjoy a full life of abundance. You can't accomplish that without having reserves that will keep you from getting wiped out during emergencies and financial challenges. With very few (and relatively inconsequential) sacrifices over time, you can set up an operational and strategic reserve that will give you peace of mind and allow you to fully enjoy the time you have with your family because you know you can make it through times of trouble. And with even smaller sacrifices—by regular, automatic contributions from your paycheck or just by not touching the principal of an investment—a tactical reserve can assist you in taking advantage of opportunity and allowing for a lifetime of wealth building.

Each of these reserves anticipates the "unexpected" in life, and we should all be dialed into the randomness of life. I know that most of the guys I served with, myself included, are dialed into the randomness of war. The very last day I was in Afghanistan, all I had left to do was to see our last group of soldiers off on a plane. At about 5 A.M., I needed to take the long walk to the bathroom facilities about 200 yards down the FOB. Any time you go outside of your hooch, you have to put on all your gear, so it took a while to get suited up. When I came out of the little johnny hut, I was letting my eyes adjust to the light, and a 105 rocket came in. You can hear them distinctly because of the noise they make, this whirling sound, almost like the rocket is spiraling. And I could tell it was close. I immediately hit the deck, and the rocket hit about 250 yards ahead of me. I started running over there, but all the people who were actually on duty to react to those things got on the scene fast, so there wasn't really anything I could do. I found out a few hours later that a civilian contractor on the base had been killed in that rocket blast. It really hit home for me because it was my last day in theatre, and in my mind I was thinking everything's safe. That rocket could have hit 250 yards my direction, and he would be the guy telling this story. You just have to know that there's going to be luck, both good and bad, on any given day, and you have to be prepared for both. If you're following a disciplined process of developing your reserves, you're more prepared for the bad luck. There's a saying: the harder I work, the luckier I get. I would say it's the same thing with investing and with the military. If you're in the right place, at the right time, in the right uniform, with the right gear and the right attitude, you're going to find, in your military career, that you get lucky a lot. In investing, if you're doing the right things, following the right fundamentals, and sticking to the right discipline, over time you're going to get lucky a lot, too. Building and sustaining a reserve is about having the willpower to keep complacency at bay, and establishing a safety net that will work to help you build a life you want in the long run.

After Action Review

If you have finished this chapter successfully and have completed the following tasks, you are hereby promoted to Specialist E-4 (SPC) in *Combat Finance*. You have:

1. Completed and maintained all key tasks from Chapter 1.
2. Consistently followed your *Combat Finance* general orders.
3. Consistently maintained your financial bearing.
4. Established your operational reserve.
5. Established your strategic reserve
6. Established tactical reserves within your long-term investment accounts.

If you have not completed each of the key tasks in this chapter, *continue reading,* but you are barred from promotion until you meet these minimum standards.

Chapter 3

Choose Your FOB Wisely

Let's face it, as Americans, we love our homes. Home ownership is considered by many to be the greatest American dream, and for the majority of us our home is our single largest asset. Our home is where we watch our children grow up, where we share time with family and friends, and it is the focal point of so many of our fondest moments. So it's no surprise that we have a tendency to want the largest, nicest home that the bank tells us that we can afford. Unfortunately, the economy's downturn has made the dream of homeownership a burden for many people. Foreclosures hit record highs in many states from 2008 to 2012, and many families were faced with the decision of whether to give up their home in the face of economic stress. As a *Combat Finance* reader, I want to help you step into a home that is right for you and your family, one that not only provides the benefits of safety, security, and personal enjoyment, but one that is also financially strong and defendable in difficult times. The purpose of this chapter is to provide you with a detailed framework for determining how much house you can actually afford. (Spoiler alert: It's less than what the lender tells you.) To accomplish this we will not only discuss some simple formulas that you can use to determine the maximum price and payment you should accept for your budget, but we will also spend some time talking about the hidden costs of owning a home. My desired end state is that you have a detailed framework for determining how much home is right for you.

FOBs, COPs, and Airfields

Military bases and homes come in many sizes and configurations that vary as greatly as the missions and families they support. Terrain, weather, and local customs and considerations all affect the location and materials that are chosen for both homes and bases. There are also many parallels that can be drawn between the cost-benefits analysis that goes into designing the right military base and the cost-benefit analysis that you should use when deciding which home you can afford to buy or build.

Airfields are the mansions of the military world. These are massive installations with anywhere from 10,000–30,000 personnel at any given time, and even though they have enormous capabilities, they're very costly to operate. A forward operating base, or FOB, is a much smaller installment. There are dozens of American FOBs in Afghanistan, and they usually contain living facilities, medical facilities, a helicopter pad, and other support facilities that allow for continuous operations. FOBs vary greatly in both size and complexity, but they are almost always designed to support a specific mission or area. In terms of manpower and resources, the more complex the FOB, the more expensive and difficult it is to defend. A Combat Outpost, or COP, is a patrol base similar to a FOB, but much smaller and with fewer capabilities and creature comforts. Troops in COPs are usually based out of a main FOB and rotated in and out so they have more access to showers, laundry, and hot meals.

Despite all the undisputed benefits of airfields, FOBs, and COPs, the more resources the military spends on these defensive positions, the fewer resources it has to go outside the wire to win the war. No conflict in history has ever been won by having the nicest facilities, and my gut tells me none ever will. A house isn't much different. If you have a home that is so large or on which you've spent so many of your resources in purchasing or running it effectively, then you don't have the resources to go out and invest your money toward wealth building. FOBs can create a very false sense of security as well. If you're constantly building and maintaining a FOB, it can feel very safe and secure. But without any offensive patrols, a FOB has many weaknesses, and the enemy needs only to wait for the right moment to make life difficult or deadly. The bottom line is that you can't win a war from the FOB, and you can't become financially independent if your home is sucking up all your income. You should purchase a home that provides for your needs, but still allows you to defend it by placing a solid portion of your income into outside savings and investments.

The Benefits of Home Ownership

There are many benefits to owning a home. Renting is fine when you are young and still building reserves, or when you have a job that moves you around frequently so you don't have time to build equity in a home, but eventually most people are better off owning. It is more difficult to get rich long term while renting because renters own nothing while buyers build equity if they buy right and spend conservatively. To build wealth, you are probably going to own some real estate. Even more important is that feeling of security that comes with building equity in a place that is yours alone. Dealing with landlords can be stressful and even financially damaging if you are evicted, don't get your deposit back, or your rent is raised. There are other reasons that homes can make great investments. Home ownership allows you to leverage the increasing value of a well-purchased piece of property. Becoming a homeowner may allow you to deduct the cost of mortgage interest every year on your taxes. Owning a home forces you to pay into your own equity each month with the portion of your mortgage that pays down principal. And traditionally, over time, home values have generally gone up. The lean years of 2006–2012 have wreaked havoc on homeowners who didn't stick to their financial bearing and overbought their homes or bought before they had their debts paid and operational and strategic reserves built, but in the long run, real estate prices have almost always gone up. To buy the right home for your budget, however, you should understand SOPs for home buying and stay true to your financial bearing. Remember, you're still following *Combat Finance* basic training and reserve principles (living debt free, maintaining an operational reserve, saving at least 10 percent of what you earn pretax, and keeping a 6- to 24-month strategic reserve) even if you purchase a home. That home has to come after those priorities, and it has to adhere to the battlefield calculus.

What is battlefield calculus? In military terms, it's a decision-making and action-planning process that takes into account all known risks and factors. It's a calculation of probability. We often use it to do force-on-force calculations to decide what our chances of winning will be. For instance, we know through experience and data that one M1 Abrams should destroy 1.6 T72s. We know this because we have an advantage with a 3,000-meter range on our weapons system with a stabilized gun, whereas T72s have a 1,000-meter range and they have to stop in order to fire, among other factors. Military bean counters figured out that although not every scenario is the same, usually one M1 up against a T72 is going to be a likely win. But if you have one M1 against 10 T72s, that would be a bad idea mathematically. The variance outside of that data will be only slight. There's only so much you can overcome with heart, enthusiasm, and training. Investors who adhere to good battlefield calculus will understand the math and know what their odds of winning will be. Does this mean that you're going to go broke if you buy a home that costs 36 percent of your take-home pay instead of 35? Not necessarily, but you are tempting fate. People who take the time to crunch the numbers will understand what the battlefield calculus is, and in turn, understand its risks and rewards.

Defending the FOB

If you ignore the battlefield calculus that we present in this chapter and go into a bigger house than you can afford, that's soup sandwich. Sure, you might get lucky, and everything will turn out okay, but if the numbers just don't pan out, then no amount of expense cutting and sacrifice on your part is going to make it work when Murphy's Law strikes. The best practice, and the one that sticks closest to good financial bearing, is to pay cash for a home. That means that you finance none of it and own it free and clear. For some homebuyers that is an option if they've been saving aggressively or saving for a long period of time. Paying for a home in cash means you're never paying interest and not wasting money that could be going toward strategic wealth building. But not everyone has that much cash saved up beyond their operating and strategic reserves.

How Much Home Can I Afford?

Annual Net Income	Monthly Net Income	35% of Monthly Net
$150,000	$12,500	$4,375
$140,000	$11,667	$4,083
$130,000	$10,833	$3,792
$120,000	$10,000	$3,500
$110,000	$9,167	$3,208
$100,000	$8,333	$2,917
$90,000	$7,500	$2,625
$80,000	$6,667	$2,333
$70,000	$5,833	$2,042
$60,000	$5,000	$1,750
$50,000	$4,167	$1,458
$40,000	$3,333	$1,167
$30,000	$2,500	$875
$20,000	$1,667	$583

(Annual Net Income/12) × .35 = 35% of Monthly Net Income
35 percent of net income is the maximum payment you should commit to, including taxes and insurance.

KEY TASK 1: Calculate how much home you can afford.

A good battlefield calculus number to use when determining your home budget is that the mortgage payment, with taxes and insurance included, should not exceed 35 percent of your *take home* (net) pay. Keep in mind, that is lower than many banks and mortgage companies will approve you for. But also bear in mind that they are primarily concerned about your ability to pay them back. Therefore, they are less concerned about whether you are investing toward your other goals, such as college education for your children or your retirement. There is a big difference between having enough to make the payments on your mortgage and having enough to make the payments on your mortgage and still achieve all your other financial goals. Use the chart to help you determine the monthly payment you can afford based on 35 percent of your take home pay. Take home pay is the pay left over after all deductions, such as income and social security taxes, health insurance, and 401(k) contributions. For example, if your monthly net income is $5,000 then you should try to keep your total monthly payment with taxes and insurance to less than $1,750. Taxes and insurance will vary by location, so check with a real estate professional in your area to help you budget accurately, but let's assume for this example that they total $350 per month. That would mean that you have $1,400 per month available for the mortgage alone, which, on a 30-year fixed mortgage at 5 percent interest, would cover an initial mortgage of approximately $260,794. With a 20 percent down payment, this would mean that you should look at homes selling for no more than $325,992.

Kuchi Home

I'm sorry, you were saying that you can't afford a nice enough home on 35 percent of your take-home pay? Even a modest home in America is envied by much of the world.

KEY TASK 2: Pay cash or put a minimum of 20 percent down on a home.

If paying cash for a home isn't possible, then you should place a 20 percent down payment to maintain your financial bearing. You should never take a loan lightly. Any debt that you accumulate will be a burden on your finances and will prevent greater wealth building with the interest you pay. But if you must take out a loan, putting at least 20 percent down allows you to minimize some of the consequences of that debt. That allows you to avoid private mortgage insurance and the interest payments on the larger loan amount. The down payment has to come from funds outside your operational and strategic reserve, and it cannot deplete it below the correct 6- to 24-month level that you calculated for yourself in the previous chapter. That means that you need to finish building your strategic reserve before you use any funds to pay for a home down payment.

How do you save for a down payment? There are several effective ways to do this. Determine how much you'll need first. The average price of an American home in 2010, for instance, cost $272,900 according to the Census Bureau. So a 20 percent down payment on the average American home would be $54,580. Once you have reviewed your budget and know what you need, create a separate savings account just for this savings goal. This account will be where you put your home savings, and it will help you avoid tapping into this money for other expenses or goals. Some banks even offer specific first-time home-buyer accounts that offer rebates on mortgage costs. Now that you have your separate savings account, you should make your savings automatic. Look at what you need to save each month and have that money transferred from your checking account into the home-buying account automatically each month when your paycheck comes in. If you never see the money, you'll never miss it. When you get closer to your savings goal, make sure you've accomplished your *Combat Finance* basic training debt elimination and that you've cut down or eliminated any other consumer loans. That will help your debt-to-credit ratio—an important factor in mortgage rates—when you finally get to purchase your home. Remember, lenders will tell you that you don't need 20 percent down and that you can use your strategic reserve for the down payment. Lenders aren't bad people, but they are in the business of selling you a loan. Allowing lenders to talk you into violating your financial bearing is like letting the enemy tell you that you only need one person in each lookout tower at night. Sure, it might work on most nights, but I can tell you from experience you'll be glad you had more security when an attack comes.

For some members of the military, a VA loan may be an option. These are loans that are guaranteed by the U.S. Department of Veterans Affairs, and they often provide wonderful interest rates and require no down payment. They also don't require private mortgage insurance, which can save you a boatload of money in the long run. This is the only exception to the 20 percent down rule in *Combat Finance*. As long as you aren't paying more than 35 percent of your take-home pay, this loan may be an option for you. Just don't allow your eligibility for a larger loan amount to blind you to the responsibilities of keeping your mortgage payments low and affordable. Remember, that a bigger house needs more furniture, costs more to heat and cool, and the tax man wants a bigger piece every year. Just because you *can* qualify for a bigger loan doesn't mean you should do it. Weigh your options, and keep your financial bearing.

KEY TASK 3: Find a 15- to 30-year fixed-rate mortgage that, with taxes and insurance, does not exceed 35 percent of your monthly take-home pay.

A 15-year mortgage is preferable, but a 30-year is acceptable if the monthly payment with taxes and insurance is less than 35 percent of your take-home income. Take-home income is not your gross, it's your *net*, so make sure you take a look at your paycheck and determine whether a specific home-payment would work. Take-home pay is your income after taxes, health insurance, 401(k) deductions, and other items that are deducted from your paycheck. A 30-year mortgage sounds great because it locks in the rate for 30 years and makes the monthly payments lower than they would be with a 15-year plan, but lenders also get rich off of 30-year mortgages. If you buy a $250,000 home at 4 percent, your mortgage payments over 30 years will wind up totaling almost $430,000. That's $180,000 in interest that you've just handed over. Imagine if you'd had that $180,000 to invest? But with a home loan, that money goes straight into the bank's pocket instead. The longer mortgage term is also a problem for people who don't live in their homes for very long. Since so many of your payments early in your mortgage go to interest and not principal, that means that if you leave your home after five years, you probably haven't paid more than a few percent toward your principal. In the first decade of a loan, nearly 90 percent of your payments are going toward interest, so you're working very hard for your bank but not so much for your own equity.

Adjustable rate mortgages, or ARMs, shouldn't be a part of your home-buying vocabulary. That's soup sandwich. If interest rates go up quickly and you have an ARM, the rate on your mortgage can go up quickly also, leaving you with trouble making unpredictable payments. You're doing the battlefield calculus in order to carefully document and understand your responsibilities as a homeowner in any situation, so finding ways to make these payments as predictable as possible is key. A typical ARM will have a set rate for the first five or seven years, and that sounds so far away when you hear advertisements for adjustable rate mortgages on the radio or TV. But think about everything that has happened in your life in the past five to seven years. I bet you're thinking that time flew by, because it does. Before you know it, the five or seven years is up and then you could find yourself with a big problem. So play it safe and go with the 15- or 30-year fixed rate. If you are following all the other *Combat Finance* rules, you'll have plenty of opportunity to take risks and make money, but risking the stability of your family's home is not the right place to do that.

"A" Way

For instance, let's look at Cindy's situation. She is a single mother of two and she works as an attorney for a government agency. She has solid job security and has been at her position for many years. Her gross income is $123,500 per year, but her take-home pay after taxes, health insurance, and other deductions is $7,510 per month. When she decided she wanted to buy a home, she found the perfect spot, a two-story Victorian, built in a suburban neighborhood, and priced at $425,000. Cindy did her homework: She knew that she had to put down $85,000, which is 20 percent of the purchase price, to avoid private mortgage insurance. She also knew that she needed to keep the $25,000 strategic reserve, which was her calculated six months of needs budget that she saved, in place when she bought the home and that she'd actually need to add to it after the purchase of her home because her monthly needs would increase. She decided that a 30-year mortgage would be best for her and, with a 5 percent interest rate, including estimates for taxes (around $125 per month) and insurance (around $80 per month), her monthly payment would be $2,500 per month. Since her take-home pay is $7,510 per month, Cindy knew that it just barely fell below 35 percent of her take-home pay maximum, which is $2,628. Cindy made an interesting choice. She decided not to purchase the home.

"It was just too much money each month for me to be able to pay into savings and wealth building," Cindy said later. "It was under the 35 percent ceiling that people told me to watch, but it was going to cut into my ability to save for a better future for my sons and me, and it was also going to be a risk for me if anything went wrong on the house or in life. It was a liability I wasn't willing to take on at the time."

Cindy eventually went on to purchase a very nice home in a better neighborhood for about $100,000 less than the one she was initially looking at. But Cindy's story provides a good illustration of why we should be conscious of the battlefield calculus when it comes to buying a home. Most lenders will limit you to a mortgage payment that (with taxes and insurance) cannot exceed 28 percent of your gross income. Or they will limit you to monthly obligations (including car payments, child support, etc.) that cannot exceed 36 percent of your gross income. But most of the people you deal with in the real estate industry will probably lack *Combat Finance* financial bearing. Again, it's not that they're bad people, but they are in the business of selling you a house, so they may not weigh the long-term goals of saving or wealth building as heavily as you should. Be overly cautious of lenders who are willing to give you large sums of money. Understand that even though you may be able to take out a loan for $500,000, you don't necessarily want to because it may overextend you and affect your ability to build-long term wealth. It can also turn a minor financial attack into a terrible day in which your FOB is overrun because you did not have the resources available to defend it. One of the most vivid examples for this analogy is COP Keating in the Nuristan region of Afghanistan, close to the village of Kamdesh.

Some Lessons from COP Keating

Combat Outpost Keating was located on low ground, near a river, and surrounded by mountains that created a giant bowl. In hindsight it was a very indefensible place to begin with. The COP originally housed a provincial reconstruction team that was tasked with projects like building roads, bridges, and schools, and it came under attack by over 250 enemy fighters on October 3, 2009. The enemy used the high ground surrounding the COP to fire down on the mortar pits, which kept the American forces from being able to fight back with one of their most effective weapon systems. Enemy combatants soon breached the wire, and a fierce battle raged within the COP. My unit was in neighboring Laghman Province, just to the west as the crow flies but with a large mountain range between us. We prepared our Quick Reaction Force for movement, but the enemy fire was too heavy for anything but gunships to fly in; due to the mountainous terrain, other units were closer by ground travel. There are several days in Afghanistan that I will never forget, and one of them is the day I listened to that fight rage over the radio from our tactical command room. I remember feeling both anger and helplessness as the events unfolded. Eight soldiers were killed, and another 22 were wounded. By the end of the day, helicopter gunships and fixed-wing aircraft were able to help U.S. ground forces retake the areas of the COP that they had lost. The soldiers at COP Keating fought with incredible bravery that day, two of them have since received the Medal of Honor for their actions. However, even their extreme courage and bravery could not completely make up for the fact that they were put in a vulnerable COP that was difficult to defend.

I tell this story because, like many battles, both military and financial, the outcome can be greatly affected by the decisions made *before* you come under attack. If you have carefully chosen a home that meets your essential needs and is very financially defensible, then you may never come under attack in the first place because the resources that you have available to commit outside the wire keeps the enemy at bay. There is a lot that can go wrong in a home and on a FOB, and we have to be able to manage those events with the appropriate amount of personnel and resources to come out on top, to deal with it successfully. I know that many of you may be thinking, "Of course it takes a lot of resources to manage a home, and of course it takes a lot of resources to defend a FOB," but what I am trying to convey is that even in your wildest imagination you cannot possibly think of all the ways that things can go wrong and force you to use more resources than you had anticipated.

Captain Soapes: FOB Mayor

As we prepared to deploy to Afghanistan we were in constant contact with the unit that we were to replace. As the executive officer of our squadron it was my job to assign personnel to cover all the administrative functions we would face in theatre. Since our unit is headquartered in Las Vegas, we get a lot of great soldiers and officers that come to us after serving on active duty and then relocate for a civilian job. One of those great officers was Captain Nick Soapes, a field artillery officer who had served previous tours in Iraq and had moved to Las Vegas to manage a security team. Captain Soapes quickly made a name for himself and was assigned as the headquarters troop commander, so it was natural that we tasked him to be our FOB mayor in theatre. FOB mayor is a title given to the person responsible for managing the operations of the base. Soapes was a skilled FOB mayor: he diplomatically handled conflicts between the 14 different military units and contracted entities on the FOB, he carefully calculated the needs of our base, and he made life as good as it could be in a war zone. Soapes compares being FOB mayor with being the superintendent for a huge apartment complex, with different families all with competing interests and competing desires that still have to work together for a common goal. It can be an overwhelming job, especially when the FOB mayor has to set and enforce the rules for everyone, including officers who outrank him.

Soapes remembers one of his most surprising challenges at FOB Mehtar Lam was a water-well system that filled into giant blivets. These blivets were like giant balloon reservoirs, and they provided water to the base. The pumps that filled them had to be manually turned on and off, so there was no automatic way of managing the water resource. He had assigned a soldier to man these blivets, to make sure they didn't get above or below a specific level. Even though that was the soldier's primary job on the base, he managed to allow them to get so full one day that they were about to explode.

"This thing was so full that I think if you even poked it with a pen it would have burst," Soapes said. "It was right next to a bunch of people's B-huts where they lived, and if it burst, it would've been the equivalent of a tsunami. It probably would've killed somebody. It was big drama until we shut the well off and started to drain it. Everything eventually got back to normal, but we needed personnel and resources to deal with that threat. It didn't just go away."

Soapes knows well the manpower it takes to manage living quarters the size of FOB Mehtar Lam. He managed essential services like water, electricity, medical supplies, and food. Anything that we take for granted living in the city is something that a FOB mayor has to manage effectively. To make the FOB work, he had to divert key warfighting manpower to managing these daily tasks, because if you don't manage the water level in the reserves, then soldiers can't shower, cook, or do laundry. He managed two giant generators to power the FOB, making sure they had enough fuel and that they were monitored. He managed a trash detail composed of local nationals. He managed security between the different American military entities and Afghans who would monitor the guard towers during the day. Soapes managed about 200 people to keep the FOB running efficiently at any given time.

Did he expect it to be such an overwhelming task? Soapes quickly learned about the time-consuming, cash-sucking elements of being a FOB mayor, but most people don't make an effort to develop and understand a detailed management plan of their own FOB, or home, before they purchase it. It's important to decide what size Combat Outpost, FOB, or airfield you can actually afford, and not just in terms of basic purchase price, but in time, manpower, and risk. A home purchase alone may make or break your wealth-building operations outside the wire. The size of your home operations will largely determine how much you have available to invest, which can be a huge limitation in your long-term financial wealth.

"I knew the job would be tough, but I didn't really know what I was getting myself into when I came," Soapes said. "I went out there early with the advance party so I could get a handle on things before everyone showed up, and I was expected to know what was going on. It was overwhelming. What was really surprising was managing people's expectations. Everyone had a demand and an expectation, and they wanted a certain quality of life. Being the problem solver I am, I went all out to solve things. But sometimes I could only do so much. We had to sit people down eventually and tell them, 'Hey, this is where we are, and this is where we want to be, and this is what we're capable of doing. So don't get your hopes up.'"

Have a Battle Plan

A roof leak, a septic burst, a heating-system failure, or other large events in homeownership can cost vast amounts of money and resources to keep your standard of living. These are often risks that homebuyers don't identify. They see a sticker price on a home and a monthly payment, but there are things like landscaping, heating bills, window coverings, and many other seemingly small expenditures and risks on a home that add to that monthly payment. You have to be prepared for these costs as well. In the military, we use detailed checklists to define our standard operating procedures for things like patrols. Our Wildhorse Patrol Book is more than 30 pages of detailed operating procedures for patrols and other recurring tasks. It details what to do in certain situations outside the wire, from combat battle drills, to ambush or IED reactions, to raids or urban patrols. Each situation is carefully documented, illustrated, and rehearsed regularly so that everyone in the 1st Squadron, 221st Cavalry is prepared to deal with anything that comes their way. All soldiers know their job and the job of the person above them, so confusion and chaos are minimized when bad things happen.

Do you have a similar battle plan for your home? Are you prepared in case the water-heater breaks, a tree on the property falls in a windstorm, or you have a termite infestation? You're going to need to know—be absolutely sure— that you're capable of defending your home in difficult times. You must know that you have the time and money to deal with these threats without dipping into your strategic reserves to do it; otherwise I want you to continue to rent and let your landlord handle these unexpected costs while you continue to build your reserves and increase your income. Remember, many costs are proportionate to the value of your home, so the more expensive a home you have, the more you pay in taxes, insurance, and special assessment districts. Other costs are proportionate to the size of your home. The larger it is, the more it will cost to heat, cool, clean, replace flooring, cover more windows, or replace a larger roof when the time comes. Even simple tasks like mowing the lawn on a weekly basis could be a drain on your resources if the lawn is many acres. You need to know that you've identified and calculated all likely expenses and still have money to save and invest outside the wire.

There are emotional considerations to home buying, and they are legitimate. You can talk about battlefield calculus and the math behind your home buying decision but many people will have an emotional attachment to a home transaction purely because of the family memories of living there. You might know that investment X is going to outperform investment Y, but investment Y fits an emotional need (as a home often does). Are you willing to sacrifice return to meet the emotional need? You truly have to marry the two concepts when you're buying a home.

A great example of this is a friend of mine and his family who purchased a beautiful lot on a golf course. They built a home on the land that was exactly what they wanted with a four-car garage and luxurious upgrades. They planned to raise their children there and stay for a long time. But when they took their young son back to their old house to pack up their things, he said he wanted to stay at the old house. It was where he was born, and the only home he'd known in his lifetime. This brought my friends to tears. At that moment, they didn't want to give up the old house even if the new one was leaps and bounds better. Of course, that emotion passed, and they love their new home, but the point is that it is perfectly normal to have a powerful emotional attachment to a home. No other financial investment is so full of impassioned pleas and poignant responses, but we always need to keep the bottom line in mind: Continue to build wealth, keep expenses low, and maintain a strategic reserve in the face of simultaneous operations. As a *Combat Finance* reader I want you to be cognizant of the emotional but concentrate on the logical side of the decision.

When I returned home from Afghanistan, it was after the financial markets had taken a turn for the worse. Many clients and friends who had been in great financial shape when I left were in dire straits when I came back. I was motivated to understand what some people did to stay afloat while others suffered, and what it eventually came down to in most of these cases was that people got in over their heads on a home purchase that drained their reserve and investments. One of these friends was at a magnificent job before I left. He made a hefty base salary, but his bonus was almost twice that. He and his wife bought a huge home and lived a lifestyle that depended heavily on his bonus payments. In 2006, when the economy began to turn, he received only half his usual bonus. Not a big deal, he thought, because he'd been receiving that bonus for nearly a decade. It would go back to normal the next year. But it didn't. By 2008, the company cut off all bonuses, and by 2009, they laid him off. To get by and pay for the large luxury home that he and his family had purchased during the flush times, he dipped into his 401(k) and worked part-time jobs when he could. By 2012, he was in bankruptcy, had gone through a divorce, and had been taking food stamps to get by.

It's a sobering story, but this friend is not alone. Many Americans faced similar fates after the economy turned. He was determined to work his way out of the hole, though. He finally found full-time work and is rebuilding, but it's a tough road for him. It's a road that would've been much easier to travel if he had owned a house that wasn't more than he could financially defend, and if he had not been complacent about the principles we discuss in this book. His FOB was not defensible. Make financial freedom a priority and you'll not only be able to enjoy your home, but you'll also be able to weather the storms that life throws at us all.

After Action Review

If you have finished this chapter successfully and have completed the following tasks you are hereby promoted to Sergeant E-5 (SGT) in *Combat Finance*. You have:

1. Completed and maintained all key tasks from previous chapters.
2. Consistently followed your *Combat Finance* general orders.
3. Consistently maintained your financial bearing.
4. Completed your consumer debt payoff plan from Chapter 1 and remained debt free.
5. Calculated and built your reserves as described in Chapter 2.
6. Used the battlefield calculus described in this chapter to budget for, save for, and purchase a home that you can defend in the face of financial attacks.

If you have not completed each of the key tasks in this chapter, *continue reading,* but you are barred from promotion until you meet these minimum standards.

Chapter 4

Me and the Sergeant Major, We Love Training

In the 2002 film, *We Were Soldiers,* Mel Gibson's grizzled character Lieutenant Colonel Hal Moore turns to his new air cavalry soldiers in a hangar and barks, "Now, I hope you men like trainin', 'cause me and the Sergeant Major, we love it!" It's a relatively accurate tribute to the training ethic in the military. As in every successful group, constant training is what keeps the military complex competitive. Battle drills, realistic simulations, and live-fire exercises conducted on a regular basis are what allow the military to live up to the uncompromising standards that we expect from our soldiers, sailors, airmen, and marines.

Financial training is just as essential in *Combat Finance*. A lot of people think they can invest for a while and then stop, that they can excel for a finite amount of time and then ignore their financial bearing while they rack up more debt or buy a car they can't afford. For some people who can build up millions in a short amount of time through an amazing business success, professional athletic talent, or an inheritance, yes, that might work. But for most people, building wealth has to be a lifelong process reinforced by constant vigilance. It has to involve effective training that reinforces the importance of regular deposits to your savings and investment accounts.

So I hope you love training, 'cause I love it! What is *Combat Finance* training? It's not just consistently living within your means and maintaining your reserves, it is also the systematic investing of a significant portion of your income on a regular, long-term basis. Successful training means that at least 10 percent of your income automatically goes into retirement accounts, investment accounts, real estate, and other financial stockpiles, no matter what you want at the mall or what confronts you in life. You've already lived through basic training and come out debt free. You've developed an operational and strategic reserve for emergencies. You've worked to build a defendable FOB. Now, you need to build regular habits of investing for retirement and for your big dreams. Financial training requires you to be constantly vigilant about setting aside money proportionately—increasing your contributions when your income increases or when you come across extra money through a gift or inheritance—to allow your money to work for you.

Those who coast and become complacent about training don't get far. Quite the opposite. Look at any successful sports team in the last few decades. A team that wins the Super Bowl one year doesn't cancel practice the next year. A college football team that wins by 35 points in their first Saturday of the season doesn't rely on last week's sprints and drills to carry them through to the next week. If they don't immediately go back to training at that high level, they don't have a chance at being a champion next week or next year.

Financial champions understand that wealth is not randomly found, nor can it be retained without solid financial bearing. In fact, people who come into a large chunk of money suddenly are statistically more likely to lose it quickly, according to a study published in *The Review of Economics and Statistics*. I believe that is because these people haven't been instilled with the necessary long-term training that's required to build and maintain wealth. If you don't train to have those principles in place to save, to invest, and to establish all the things we've talked about in basic training and throughout *Combat Finance*, if you don't work so hard to make those habits part of your daily life, then those principles certainly won't stick when there is money to spare.

The Power of Compound Returns

The power of investing is transformative. Consider this hypothetical example for a moment so that you can understand the mathematical potential of long-term compound returns. If you contributed $5,000 per year into an investment account beginning at the age of 20 and your investment received a 10 percent pretax compounded return every year, you would have more than $1 million in that account by the time you're 51. If you were able to continue to earn that hypothetical 10 percent per year pretax total return, that $1 million would earn about $100,000 each year. Think about the ramifications of that. It means that if you can live off of that amount, after holding back taxes and reinvesting some of the earnings to keep up with inflation over the long term, then you are financially independent just after turning 51. But that initial $5,000 contribution per year doesn't always come easy. It can be tempting to ignore it for short-term wants, especially in years where the market performs poorly or in the early years when the returns don't seem to make much difference. After all, if you get a 10 percent return on your first $5,000, your account will only go up by $500, and most people don't get too excited about that. But the same 10 percent return later, when your account is $50,000 is now a $5,000 gain, and that looks a little better. Then by the time your account is at $500,000, and a 10 percent gain is $50,000, you're a huge fan of training and want to yell it from the mountaintop. Now please don't set the book down and say that I guaranteed you would earn 10 percent per year and that you would have $500,000 in your account because that is not the point. The point is that successful *Combat Finance* readers know that good financial bearing means forgoing some of the things on their want list to build for a better financial future. Good financial bearing means remembering to be vigilant about your finances each day of the year. That's the power of focused, consistent training, and that's the power of Compound Returns.

Although I just discussed a hypothetical scenario involving a 10 percent compound rate of return, I think it is important to note that a 7 percent pretax return on a diversified portfolio of investments over a long term is much more likely. Having said that, you should never count on drawing that much from your accounts in retirement or for living expenses. I think it is much more prudent that people count on a maximum draw from a diversified investment portfolio of no greater than 4 percent if they don't want to deplete the principal and purchasing power of the account over time. If, over the long haul of 10 to 30 years, we see someone averaging a 10 percent pretax return—which is possible for someone who has aggressively invested—that's great, but 6 or 7 percent is more likely for a diversified portfolio. If we draw 4 percent from that, the additional 2 to 3 percent that stays in that account allows for keeping up with inflation. Even if you're earning a higher pretax return on an aggressive account, never draw more than 4 percent from it per year so that you have a better chance of sustaining yourself through the down years. Consider that part of your *Combat Finance* training.

The Blackhorse Regiment Knows Training

One great example of effective training is the story of the 11th Armored Cavalry Regiment (ACR) in Fort Irwin, California. The 11th Armored Cavalry Regiment, or the Blackhorse Regiment, which is the parent company to our squadron, the 1-221 Cavalry, was formed in 1901 for service in the Philippine campaign. After distinguished service in Vietnam and Germany, the regiment was tasked to be an opposing force at the National Training Center at Fort Irwin. Just about every brigade-level unit within the army has to cycle through the National Training Center about once every four years. They move all their troops, supplies, and resources in on railroad cars, and they set up as they would in a war zone to face a simulated enemy. The opposing forces at Fort Irwin work every day to help other units train using realistic fighting simulations in the middle of the Mojave desert. Our unit cycled in to this opposing-forces role dozens of times during my service in the Nevada National Guard, and we always took our mission very seriously in an effort to make the fighting as real as possible for other units who faced us. Currently, the unit simulates fighting in Iraq or Afghanistan and it is very realistic.

We would set up shop-front ambushes, exploding IEDs, and mock riots among the native speakers of Pashto, Dari, and Pashie. There were goats roaming the simulated streets where shopkeepers sold bread. They even hired a Hollywood set company to build streets, buildings, and landscape that look exactly as they would in theatre. It's a realistic setup that immerses forces in counterinsurgency warfare. The 11th ACR has a unique mission because they have to artificially reinforce the importance of training for other units. In other words, they have to win. The goal is to have other units come in, face these opposing forces, and leave with a commitment to train harder because they lost. And the 11th ACR doesn't just win; they have a reputation for kicking the snot out of other units. The culture has to include being the best in every simulated battle, to provide a forceful and overwhelming opposing force that leaves other units scrambling to train more, and to increase their level of proficiency. We must do this to make sure that each unit is so well prepared and so motivated to improve their training that it reduces or eliminates the likelihood of casualties or lapses in judgment in theatre.

The reason I want to focus on this is that all military units are constantly training. Without training, complacency builds. You could have a fully trained unit that's capable of executing a mission, such as the top-notch Navy SEALs that took down Osama bin Laden, but if they stop training, that ability to act at a high level starts deteriorating. Even if you're training, but not as hard, you lose that edge. There are a lot of lessons that this kind of military training ethic can teach us about why we save and invest. We don't scrimp and save just to scrimp and save, or because we have taken some sort of poverty vow to train at all costs. We save now so that we have an incredibly rich world of opportunity available to us that we would never have if we are always living paycheck to paycheck, no matter how big that paycheck is.

Make Investment Automatic

There are easy ways to maintain the kind of training that results in the systematic investment of a minimum 10 percent of your income. You have to make it simple and automatic. A good example of how we do that in the military is the way we automatically schedule physical training each morning before we do anything else. It makes physical training automatic, and although it's not always easy, it takes any thought out of the decision to do it. Investment training will require the same automation. We'll use two key tasks in this chapter to establish effective financial training.

KEY TASK 1: Establish retirement investments.

The first step in setting up your retirement savings is to figure out which retirement accounts are available to you and, of those, which will provide the greatest benefit. Some are only sponsored through an employer, such as 401(k)s, 403(b)s, 457 plans, SEP-IRAs and SIMPLE IRAs, profit-sharing accounts, and money purchase plans. Others, such as individual IRAs and Roth IRAs, are available to most people even if your employer does not offer a retirement plan. The options are vast, so my objective is to help you figure out which combination will have the best chance to maximize the benefits for you and your family. Everyone's individual situation is unique, and that's why in coming chapters I will make a strong case for working with competent advisors, but in the meantime you can refer to Table 4.1 to see which types of plans might be available and the maximum dollar limits you are allowed to place in each. Then use the diagram in Figure 4.1 to help you choose which ones might be right for you and your family based on availability, the existence of an employer match, and so on.

The first thing I want you to find out is if you have a retirement plan at work and if they will match any part of your contributions. Why is this so important? Let's do the math. If you are single and you make between \$36,250 and \$87,850 of adjusted gross income in 2013, you'll pay 25 cents of each dollar you earn in taxes. So for every dollar that you don't put in your 401(k), you're only taking home 75 cents of it. Now, if instead of taking that in a paycheck each month, you divert it into a retirement account, the government does not tax that investment until you retire. So your 75 cents just turned into a whole dollar right there. If your employer matches that dollar, you've turned that original 75 cents of take home pay into \$2 in your 401(k). That is a huge return on the 75 cents you would have kept after taxes. The math is so simple, yet so many people fail to take advantage of the free

Table 4.1 Maximum Dollar Limits

	2013	2012	2011
Annual employee contribution limit for 401(k), 403(b), or 457 savings plans	$17,500	$17,000	$16,500
Annual catch-up contribution limit for 401(k), 403(b), or 457 savings plans if employee is age 50 or over	$5,500	$5,500	$5,500
Maximum annual benefit payable by a defined benefit pension plan	$205,000	$200,000	$195,000
Annual limit for combined employer-employee contributions to a defined contribution plan	$51,000	$50,000	$49,000
Annual contribution limit to an Individual Retirement Account for individuals	$5,500	$5,000	$5,000
Annual catch-up contribution limit for Individual Retirement Accounts for individuals age 50 or over	$1,000	$1,000	$1,000
Annual employee contribution for SIMPLE plans	$12,000	$11,500	$11,500
Annual catch-up employee contribution for SIMPLE plans if employee is age 50 or over	$2,500	$2,500	$2,500

Amounts provided by IRS.gov, accessed March 25, 2013.

money being offered by their employer. That's soup sandwich. As a *Combat Finance* reader I want you to take free money when you can get it, so you will maximize any legitimate retirement plan match that your employer offers. For example, if your employer matches your contributions dollar for dollar up to a maximum 3 percent of your pay, then I want you to contribute at least 3 percent so that you get the full match. Another employer might match 50 cents of every dollar that you contribute up to 5 percent of your pay. In that case, I want you to contribute at least 5 percent so that you get the full match, even if you're still building your strategic reserve or paying down debts. Keep in mind that you will pay taxes on the money when you take it out in retirement and there are penalties on most withdrawals before you turn 59½ , but since this is long-term retirement money and not your operational or strategic reserves, that shouldn't be a problem.

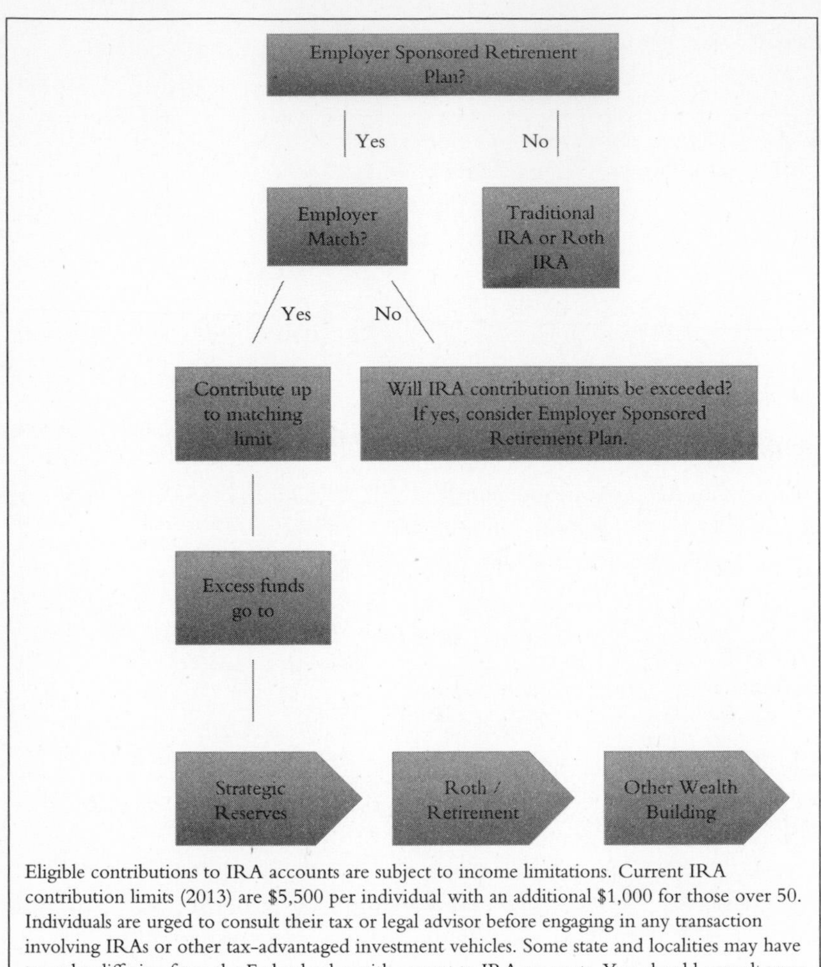

Figure 4.1 Maximum Dollar Limits

There are other things to consider such as vesting schedules, fees, expenses, and investment selections. A vesting schedule details the period of time that you must remain working for the company to retain all or a portion of the employer match (see Figure 4.2). For example, a common vesting schedule is a graduated five-year plan, such that you keep 20 percent of the match if you leave after one year, 40 percent if you leave after two, and so forth until you are 100-percent vested if

Example of a typical five-year vesting schedule for an employer sponsored plan.

Total of employee contributions (10%)	$6,000
Total of employer match contributions (5%)	$3,000
Grand total of all 1st year contributions	$9,000

Typical Five-Year Vesting Schedule

Year	Percentage of Employer Match Vested	Total Fully Vested
1	20% of $3,000 = $600	$6,600
2	40% of $3,000 = $1,200	$7,200
3	60% of $3,000 = $1,800	$7,800
4	80% of $3,000 = $2,400	$8,400
5	100% of $3,000 = $3,000	$9,000

Above calculations assume a $60,000 annual salary, 10 percent employee contribution, and 5 percent employer matching contribution for a single year. As annual contributions are made, not only will the account balance have a potential to grow, but all employer contributions are fully vested after the fifth year. Employee contributions are always fully vested.

Figure 4.2 Sample Vesting Schedule

you remain with the company for five years or more. Other companies provide 100-percent vesting either right away or after a short period, such as six months. As long as the vesting, fees, expenses, and investment selections are reasonable, it only makes sense to start your retirement investments by taking advantage of your employer's matching contributions. Once you are contributing at least the full amount that will be matched, and you have paid off all debts, built your reserves, and purchased a reasonable home, then you can decide where to invest the rest of the 10 percent or more that you are setting aside every paycheck.

ROTH IRAs

Now, you already know I love training, but I also have an affinity for Roth IRAs. After sliced bread and free money from your employer match, a Roth ranks right up there. The reason is that as long as you wait until you are 59½ years old, your earnings on a Roth IRA can be taken out tax free. That makes it a great account to complement your employer plan once you have maximized the amount they will match. As of 2013, Roth IRAs allow you to contribute up to $5,500 per year, per person, subject to certain limitations such as income caps. In addition, there is a catch-up rule that allows you to contribute an additional $1,000 per year if you are 50 years of age or older. Investments purchased inside your ROTH grow tax-free as long as you leave it in there until retirement age. So if you contribute $5,500 per year for 36 years and you earn an 8 percent total pretax return, you'll have over $1 million that can be taken out tax free when you retire. In that situation, you would've invested only $150,000 to make that $1 million; the rest is just your money working for you through the power of compound returns. And since you pay no taxes on the withdrawal, it can be a great addition to your employer's retirement accounts.

Think about how it will work if you follow the *Combat Finance* plan. You are debt-free with your house paid off by retirement, and then, since you contributed to your employer plan to get the match and you contributed to a Roth IRA, you can now determine your lifestyle. You can collect your social security or military pension to provide some nice monthly income, and you can set your Thrift Savings Plan (TSP) or employer-sponsored plan to give you a certain amount each month to supplement the social security or pension. Then you have your Roth that you can draw from as needed to pay for big things such as replacing a car, because taking money out of the Roth won't increase your taxable income and push you into a higher tax bracket in retirement. So start your retirement contributions by making the most of any employer match you can get, and then look at other savings options for the rest of your minimum 10 percent retirement contribution.

Never Go to Battle without a Plan

Remember, 10 percent of your income toward investing is just a minimum. If you start investing early enough, that will likely provide for a reasonably comfortable level of financial independence later in life. However, like any important endeavor in life, *Combat Finance* readers don't just wing it, we plan. Be sure you calculate how many years you have left until retirement, the amount you want to retire with, and whether your regular contribution into your retirement savings account will be enough to reach this goal. For instance, let's say you're a 45-year-old plumber who makes $80,000 per year. Maybe you've procrastinated and haven't contributed anything to a retirement account yet. That's soup sandwich, but now that you are a *Combat Finance* reader, let's figure out the math to get you on the right track. If you would like to retire at 65 with $1 million in savings, you'll need to contribute more than the minimum 10 percent into that account each month. With a 10 percent pretax return on your contributions, you'll need to contribute 20 percent of your income each month to that retirement account to get to your $1 million goal. Be sure to take the time to review your goals and then calculate the amount you will need to save to get there so that you have a solid plan. We are going to cover this kind of planning in detail in Chapter 8, so don't fret about it too much here. In the meantime, just remember that hope is not an acceptable strategy.

For most of us, our financial assets need to be diversified. It would be a mistake in most cases to have all your investments in a retirement account. You can't invest in other projects if all your money is tied up in an account that you can't touch (without penalty) until you're 59½. So I often suggest that once your employer match is met, then the rest of your minimum 10 percent of your income that you invest may be better served by contributing to other accounts such as college savings, general wealth building, or a big dream account. These investment accounts are separate from your operational and strategic reserve accounts, and they are usually allocated differently from your retirement account because they have a different objective. But, like any effective training program, you must be consistent, so you should contribute to them regularly and automatically, just as you do for your retirement account. How do you do that effectively? You make it easy on yourself.

KEY TASK 2: Make contributions to your savings and investment accounts automatic.

If you have to manually go into your checking account and transfer money from your paycheck into your savings and investment accounts, there is no way you will do that on a regular basis. It's too hard. The best way to train yourself to make savings a habit is to get your minimum 10 percent out of your operational account before you ever see it. That way, you can't mentally spend it before you contribute to building your own wealth first. Most banks allow you to set up an automatic transfer from your account on the day your paycheck is deposited. So if you know that your paycheck goes into your checking account on the first day of every month, then you can set up transfers to your retirement account and your big dream account on that same day so the money is contributed before you even see it. Some banks and employers even allow you to contribute a percentage of your paycheck instead of a dollar amount, which is even better. That will force your contribution to your savings to increase proportionally each time you get a raise. Any time you receive a raise, you should always increase your savings amounts by 50 percent of that raise. This won't even register for you, I promise. You'll still be getting more money in your paycheck than you're used to, and if you're used to eating ramen every day, moving up to boxed macaroni and cheese will still really rock.

You need to also train yourself to contribute 50 percent of any found money to these accounts. Any time you receive a chunk of money in your tax returns, in a bonus, or if you win a hole-in-one contest at the local golf tournament, put half of that into your savings. This kind of automatic commitment to training—you don't think twice, you just know that this money is going into your savings account—is what makes a successful *Combat Finance* investor. These contributions will become a permanent part of your financial bearing, making saving systematic over time.

Combat Finance Professional Development (CFPD)

Combat Finance readers, welcome to your first *Combat Finance* Professional Development training. What is CFPD you ask? That is a great question. If you have completed all tasks in the first three chapters, you were promoted to the rank of Sergeant E-5(SGT) at the end of Chapter 3. This means you are now a *Combat Finance* non-commissioned officer and with that comes great pride, authority, and respect but also certain responsibilities and commitments. In the military, one of those commitments is to further your pursuit of the profession of arms by conducting and attending Non-Commissioned Officer Professional Development (NCOPD) training. This training is usually conducted at the unit level and is in addition to the traditional branch schools that are required for promotion to E-6, E-7, and so forth. Often, it will consist of a keynote address from a senior NCO or officer who will discuss lessons learned and provide advice and insights to the unit's NCOs. So today we have a real treat for all of you *Combat Finance* readers, because our first CFPD will feature Sergeant Major of the Army (SMA) Retired, Kenneth O. Preston. SMA (R) Preston is a former 11th Armored Cavalry Regiment Trooper and member of the Blackhorse Association like me, so he agreed to answer some questions about his experiences in the military and how those lessons helped him secure his family's financial future. Read on and you'll get some great advice and mentorship from one of the army's finest NCOs.

Name: Sergeant Major of the Army (SMA) (R) Kenneth O. Preston
Total years of service: 36
Rank: SMA (R)
Combat Deployments:

Operation(s)	**Year(s)**	**Unit Served**
Operation Positive Force	April–September 1991	A Troop, 11th ACR
Operation Desert Strike	September–December 1996	3rd Battalion 8th Cavalry &1st Cavalry
Kosovo	June 2000–April 2001	1st Armored Division
Kuwait/Iraq	November 2002–December 2003	V Corps/CJTF-7

KN: SMA Preston, that is quite an impressive career of service. How old were you when you first began your military service, and what branch did you choose?
KP: *I enlisted at age 18 in the army as an Armor Crewman.*

KN: So you did your basic training at Fort Knox, Kentucky, which was, until recently, the home of the U.S. Army Armor

School. Thinking back to basic training, describe some of your experiences.

KP: *My drill sergeant in basic training at Fort Knox while assigned to A Co, 11th Battalion, 5th Training Brigade was SFC Dailey, a Vietnam Infantry Soldier, highly decorated and a great role model and leader. Before our current trend of making the training in basic training the challenge versus the drill sergeant, SFC Dailey was one of those leaders who did not have to get in your face or yell and scream. I was very fortunate to have him as a first role model. After eight weeks of basic training I received eight weeks of Advanced Individual Training as an Armor Crewman at Fort Knox while assigned to D Company, 3rd Battalion, 1st Training Brigade. My drill sergeant was SFC Underwood, also a seasoned senior NCO, who was a Vietnam veteran and a great role model.*

KN: It sounds like you had some great mentors in the army right from day one. Which values have you learned in the military that have made you a better person?

KP: *I've lived the seven army values of loyalty, duty, respect, selfless service, honor, integrity, and personal courage. As a soldier and the SMA, we ensured these values were captured in the Soldier's Creed.*

KN: Outstanding, that's great stuff, Sergeant Major Preston, because those same values can lead to financial success as well. How has your military experience shaped your approach to your personal finances?

KP: *The military, especially while serving as a noncommissioned officer and leader in a wide variety of assignments, has taught me to be prepared for a wide variety of missions, opportunities, and what the enemy might execute. Applying these principles toward my personal finances, I never knew when my military career would end, and I would have to make a transition to a new career. My goal with my military career was to be financially independent and grow my wealth to achieve a greater quality of life for my family and me.*

KN: Sergeant Major Preston, would you tell us about the proudest moment of your military career, and how do you think it has affected you?

KP: *There have been many proud moments. All three of my children were born into the military lifestyle, and their presence has kept me focused on my missions in the army and balancing my army career with my life at home.*

Serving as the V Corps CSM and working alongside then–Lieutenant General William S. Wallace and all the senior leaders in the 170,000-man task force during the invasion into Iraq was a great honor. Continuing to serve with Lieutenant General Ricardo Sanchez and the CJTF-7 team for the first year in Iraq was an experience I will always treasure. With having great power while assigned to these positions comes great responsibility. I never take any mission or assignment for granted, nor the people who work in my care.

KN: If you would, please tell us about the most difficult moment or experience in your military career and how do you think it affected you?

KP: *There have been many times during my career when I was asked to do a mission above and beyond what I believed to be the scope of my abilities, or asked to step up and take on the increased responsibilities of an assignment knowing the work and commitment that would be needed to succeed. Reflecting back on all those assignments, it was the commitment to selfless service that put the mission before self and family. I have no regrets.*

KN: Thank you so much for sharing that with us, Sergeant Major Preston. On a lighter note, what was the funniest or most embarrassing moment of your military career? What did you learn from that experience?

KP: *My most embarrassing moment was while serving as a sergeant and the gunner on the platoon leader's tank. After walking off the graduation stage at the Basic NCO course, I found my platoon leader had been compassionately reassigned to another installation. I was now the tank commander of our tank with my driver now serving as the gunner and a mechanic serving as the driver. When I joined the crew, we were in the process of shooting Tank Table VI, and I had four days to train a crew before Tank Table VIII qualification. We failed to qualify on that first run, and I lived under the cloud of failure for the next year.*

What I learned from this experience was that I never wanted to fail at anything again.

Sergeant Major Preston, thank you so much for answering these questions and for your outstanding service to the United States army and our nation. You provided some great insight and mentorship to our *Combat Finance* community regarding what it takes to lead, not only in our careers but in our personal financial lives as well. You mentioned having great mentors, being prepared for whatever the enemy might do, and balancing work and family. These are all great things that help us expand our professional knowledge and bring depth to our experiences. All of which give us greater wisdom to reach our goal of financial freedom. Thank you again for your time with us and your service, Sergeant Major Preston.

Combat Finance readers, you can look forward to more CFPD as you move to the next chapters.

Compound Returns, Part Deux

Why do we want saving and investing to be a permanent habit? I regularly use one story when I'm talking to clients to illustrate the importance of saving over time, or in other parlance, building capital. It's a story about a ditch digger. Let's say you have a recent high-school graduate, a 17-year-old with few skills who needs to enter the workforce. Let's say he takes a job for someone who needs to have a ditch dug, and maybe he gets paid $10 for every cubic yard of ditch he digs. If we need a ditch three feet deep and three feet wide and three feet long, he'll get $10. If he's in a place with little capital and no tools, he'll need to dig that first ditch with his bare hands, so he might get one cubic yard done in a day. That's $10 per day. But let's say he's a smart *Combat Finance* reader and he is able to sustain himself on only $5 per day. That means he's saving up the other half of that income each day so that after a few days of work he can go buy a shovel. Then with a shovel he might be able to dig three times as much ditch in a single day. Now he's making $30 per day. In this case, the capital (the shovel) combined with the labor increases his productivity;

the higher the productivity, the higher the standard of living. He could continue to save half his income each paycheck and eventually buy a backhoe. Imagine all the ditches he could dig with a backhoe, maybe 100 cubic yards. Now he's earning $1,000 per day. That's a simplistic way of understanding that there is a direct relationship between capital and productivity. The more capital you have, the more productive your labor can be and the higher your standard of living. When you save and invest that minimum of 10 percent—preferably closer to 15 or 20 percent—of your income, what you're doing is increasing the size of your capital. You're buying that shovel, you're buying that backhoe, and then you're buying an entire construction crew as you build more and more capital. And that capital starts earning money for you. A quote that has been attributed to Ben Franklin puts it this way, "Money begets money, and its offspring begets more still." Of course, your capital (money) might be in the form of assets in a 401(k), or a rental property, or even a small business, but the concept is the same.

Someone once said that compound interest is the eighth wonder of the world—a quote attributed to different sources from Ben Franklin to Albert Einstein to Baron Rothschild. Whoever said it was right on, but the greatest power is in the hands of the people who truly understand how it works and set it to work for them. There's never been an easier way to see the power of compound interest, and why you should start investing as soon as possible, than by looking at the time value of money. Let's say Investor A decides to start throwing $5,000 per year into a retirement account when she is 19. She's working her way through college and has scrimped and saved just over $400 per month that she diverts into an account that earns a 10 percent return, compounded each year. Let's say she does really great until she turns 27, at which point she is just partying too much and she forgets to ever contribute to her retirement account ever again. She just drops it. Yes, that is soup sandwich, but bear with me for a minute so you can see why this is an important example. Now, let's look at Investor B. Maybe he has a tough time finding professional work after college and really doesn't make retirement a priority until he lands his first real job at 27. He's ecstatic and finally feels like he has enough money to set aside $5,000 per year in the same kind of account as Investor A. He's working his butt off each year, putting that $5,000 away for 38 years until

The Time Value of Money*

Invest Now Rather Than Later

INVESTOR A INVESTING AT AGE 19			INVESTOR B INVESTING AT AGE 27		
AGE	INVESTMENT	TOTAL VALUE	AGE	INVESTMENT	TOTAL VALUE
19	$5,000	$5,500	19	0	0
20	$5,000	$11,550	20	0	0
21	$5,000	$18,205	21	0	0
22	$5,000	$25,526	22	0	0
23	$5,000	$33,578	23	0	0
24	$5,000	$42,436	24	0	0
25	$5,000	$52,179	25	0	0
26	$5,000	$62,897	26	0	0
27	0	$69,187	27	$5,000	$5,500
28	0	$76,106	28	$5,000	$11,550
29	0	$83,716	29	$5,000	$18,205
30	0	$92,088	30	$5,000	$25,526
31	0	$101,297	31	$5,000	$33,578
32	0	$111,427	32	$5,000	$42,436
33	0	$122,569	33	$5,000	$52,179
34	0	$134,826	34	$5,000	$62,897
35	0	$148,309	35	$5,000	$74,687
36	0	$163,140	36	$5,000	$87,656
37	0	$179,454	37	$5,000	$101,921
38	0	$197,399	38	$5,000	$117,614
39	0	$217,139	39	$5,000	$134,875
40	0	$238,853	40	$5,000	$153,862
41	0	$262,738	41	$5,000	$174,749
42	0	$289,012	42	$5,000	$197,724
43	0	$317,913	43	$5,000	$222,996
44	0	$349,704	44	$5,000	$250,795
45	0	$384,675	45	$5,000	$281,375
46	0	$423,142	46	$5,000	$315,012
47	0	$465,456	47	$5,000	$352,014
48	0	$512,002	48	$5,000	$392,715
49	0	$563,202	49	$5,000	$437,487
50	0	$619,522	50	$5,000	$486,735
51	0	$681,475	51	$5,000	$540,909
52	0	$749,622	52	$5,000	$600,500
53	0	$824,584	53	$5,000	$666,050
54	0	$907,043	54	$5,000	$738,155
55	0	$997,747	55	$5,000	$817,470
56	0	$1,097,522	56	$5,000	$904,717
57	0	$1,207,274	57	$5,000	$1,000,689
58	0	$1,328,001	58	$5,000	$1,106,258
59	0	$1,460,801	59	$5,000	$1,222,383
60	0	$1,606,882	60	$5,000	$1,350,122
61	0	$1,767,570	61	$5,000	$1,490,634
62	0	$1,944,327	62	$5,000	$1,645,197
63	0	$2,138,759	63	$5,000	$1,815,217
64	0	$2,352,635	64	$5,000	$2,002,239
65	0	$2,587,899	65	$5,000	$2,207,963

SEE THE DIFFERENCE

Earnings beyond Investment
$2,547,899

Earnings beyond Investment
$2,012,963

Investor A's Earnings	$2,547,899
Investor B's Earnings	$2,012,963
	$534,936

*Assumptions: Contributions of $5,000 made every January 2nd and assumes a 10 percent annual rate of return. This example is used for illustrative purposes only and is not meant to depict performance of any specific investment. Systematic investing does not assume a profit or protect against loss in declining markets.

his retirement at age 65. Want to see the true power of the time value of money and compound interest? Despite contributing for 30 more years than Investor A, Investor B will have $534,936 less in his account by retirement age. Investor A, having contributed for a while and then left the principal of her money alone for 30 years will have $2,547,899 to Investor B's $2,012,963. Now let's look at a *Combat Finance* reader. If that reader, who started reading this book in her teens because she cares about her financial future, starts at 19 and puts away $5,000 per year into her investment account all the way until she is 65, she will have over $4 million. That's the power of capital, and that's the power of allowing your money to work for you. Start as early as you can. Make that a commitment to yourself each year until you retire. Don't wait, begin now. It helps to focus on the idea that you don't want to be sitting around seven years from now in the same spot you're in now because you chose not to act. Whether you are 19 or 39 or 59, start training today so that you have the best future possible. Then teach your kids about how to manage money so that they can be the ones who start at age 19.

After Action Review

If you have finished this chapter successfully and have completed the following tasks, you are hereby promoted to Staff Sergeant E-6 (SSG) in *Combat Finance*. You have:

1. Completed and maintained all key tasks from previous chapters.
2. Consistently followed your *Combat Finance* general orders.
3. Consistently maintained your financial bearing.
4. Completed your consumer debt payoff plan from Chapter 1 and remained debt-free.
5. Calculated and built your reserves as described in Chapter 2.
6. Used the battlefield calculus described in Chapter 3 to budget for, save, and purchase a home that you can defend in the face of financial attacks.
7. Established retirement and big dream accounts by investing *at least* 10 percent of your income and made it automatic through payroll deduction or an automated weekly or monthly bank transfer.

If you have not completed each of the key tasks in this chapter, *continue reading,* but you are barred from promotion until you meet these minimum standards.

Chapter 5

Protect the Home Front

In America, the financial journey is depicted as an offensive one. The TV image of shouting men aggressively trading stocks and wagering on the markets is what some people associate with financial success. Yes, that offensive effort can be one component to our economic journey, but we can't win the financial war without solidifying our defensive position as well. A great way to understand the importance of a defensive stronghold in any dominant force is to look at the United States Coast Guard. The Coast Guard is tasked with our nation's safety and security. They have specific forces and personnel that work not to win the war overseas, but to protect the home front. The Coast Guard's mission—to protect maritime interests, aid navigation, provide search and rescue, guard environmental interests, defend marine safety, ready the home defense, and insulate against drug trade—is inherently so defensive that in 2003 they were transferred to the Department of Homeland Security.

The Coast Guard's motto is "Semper Paratus," which means "Always Ready," signaling their preparation for anything on the home front that might pop up. And stuff does pop up. It doesn't matter how great our military is: If the borders of our home front aren't properly defended, we could face a disaster that would make all our offensive efforts for naught. An example of that would be the events of September 11, 2001. The United States lost more people in that attack on our soil than we've lost soldiers in our entire decade-long offensive battle in Afghanistan. It's important not to forget to protect the home front, or it can be more dangerous than wartime operations outside the wire. These offensive and defensive battles should be synchronized and complement one another; they are very distinct and different in their objectives.

Insurance

The way we defend our home front in our battle for financial independence is through insurance. Insurance is a defensive method of managing risk by hedging against uncertain events that can cause large or catastrophic loss. There are many different ways of accomplishing this. In the case of life insurance, for example, the policy provides a sum of money for the family to maintain their lifestyle in the case that the main breadwinner loses his or her life. Car insurance protects against complete transportation loss. Disability insurance provides income if you're unable to work.

Although insurance is necessary, at its core it's not an investment. It is not meant to be an offensive strategy. Sometimes insurance agents succeed at convincing people to combine investments with insurance, but this is rarely a good idea. What they end up getting is a decent insurance policy tucked alongside an ill-performing, high-fee investment that could work better for them invested elsewhere. It's important to keep the offensive and defensive battle operations coordinated, but separate. Investments are there to help us achieve our goals and dreams through wealth building, while insurance makes sure we aren't devastated in the case of a disaster at home. Insurance will help protect against loss, but investments are monies put forth for offensive return.

There are four main categories of insurance that we will discuss for our defensive operations: (1) property and casualty, (2) life, (3) health, and (4) disability. Property and casualty insurance protects homes, cars, and businesses. Property insurance protects a person or business with an interest in physical property against the loss of property or the income-producing abilities of the property. Casualty insurance protects against legal liability for losses caused by injury to other people or damage to the property of others. Life insurance supports dependents if you die prematurely. Health insurance covers you if you're seriously ill, and disability insurance helps pay your bills if you are disabled and cannot work. Of course these are very simple explanations, so let's take a moment to look a little closer at the different kinds of insurance.

Insurance—What Is It?

There are many types of insurance: home, vehicle, life, disability, and health. The main purpose of any type of insurance is to transfer risk. Although there are laws requiring you to maintain insurance on your vehicles, no such requirement is in place for life, disability or long-term care, yet they are vital to your financial success. Let's take a look at each type of insurance.

Life

There are two major types of life insurance, term and permanent. Term life insurance covers you for a specific period of time. Term does not have any value, except for the death benefit. Term insurance is very affordable and can be tailored to your specific needs in terms of death benefit and time period. Permanent life insurance can most commonly be found in the form of whole life, variable, and universal. Unlike term, a permanent life policy has a cash surrender value that you receive if you ever cancel your policy. This cash value can be withdrawn at any time before you die. Because of this feature, permanent life insurance also acts like a savings vehicle. This feature causes permanent life policies to be more expensive than term life.

The amount of insurance that one needs is determined by what you want the insurance to accomplish for your survivors. Do you want to pay off the mortgage, pay for your kids to go to college, or provide income for your spouse? Weighed against the benefits of the policy will be the cost. Although there are many guidelines about how much insurance is appropriate, I recommend that a policy cover a minimum of 10 times the annual household gross income for the main breadwinner in the family. Life insurance should also be considered for nonworking spouses because of the value that they bring to the family. Although they may not earn a paycheck, replacing their skills at home (cooking, cleaning, child care, and so on) would be expensive. For this reason, I recommend that the minimum coverage for the non-breadwinner be based on five times the annual household gross income.

Disability

Disability insurance is designed to replace your income should you suffer an injury that prevents you from working. This is especially important if you are the main breadwinner of the family. I recommend that a minimum of 60 percent of the gross annual income for all adult earners be a minimum guide. There are two types of disability insurance, short-term and long-term. Short-term disability provides income replacement, usually after one week of disability, and pays for a period of up to six months. Long-term disability provides income replacement after six months and continues until age 65. The cost of disability insurance is determined by the features of the plan to include:

- *Waiting period.* The shorter the waiting period, the higher the premium.
- *Amount of benefit.* The higher the amount, the higher the premium.
- *Duration of benefit.* The longer the duration, the higher the premium.

It should be noted that if you pay the premiums for disability insurance, the benefits are tax-free. If your employer pays the premiums, the benefits are taxed as regular income.

Long-Term Care (LTC)

Long-term-care (LTC) insurance is designed to help pay for your care should you be unable to care for yourself. A misconception is that Medicare or health-care insurance will pay for care in a nursing facility.

These expenses, which can run anywhere from $4,000 to $6,500 per month, are paid via self-pay, LTC insurance, or Medicaid. However, keep in mind that to qualify for Medicaid, you have to deplete all your resources (with the exception of your primary residence and one vehicle). The cost of LTC varies depending on your age, amount of coverage, length of benefits, and current health.

Like all insurance products, the amount of coverage, the length of coverage, the elimination period, your age, and any other benefits that may be added determine the premium that is paid for LTC. LTC not only covers assistance at a living facility, but also in-home care by skilled and unskilled help. However, all policies differ in the amount and length of coverage, and great care should be taken to fully understand your individual policy.

Homeowner's Insurance

As a homeowner, you want to protect your property from damage and destruction. A homeowner's policy protects the structure, any out buildings, and your possessions within. Many natural disasters such as wind damage, hail, and fire are covered by your typical homeowner's insurance policy. However, you should confirm with your insurance agent what is and what is not covered by your particular policy.

It should be noted that floods and earthquakes are not covered by your homeowner's policy. These two natural disasters are covered only by special policies specific to flooding and earthquakes. Policies are issued by private companies and from government programs.

A homeowner's insurance policy not only protects the home and its contents, but also offers liability coverage for the owners as a result of an injury on the property or as a result of actions by the owner. Policies have varying liability limits, and therefore it is recommended that you consult your insurance representative to assure that those limits are sufficient for your needs.

Renter's Insurance

If you are not a homeowner and are currently renting, you should consider renter's insurance. Although your landlord may have an insurance policy in place to protect the structure, it does not cover the articles that belong to the renter. Renter's insurance covers your belongings within the rented premises.

If you do not have sufficient emergency funds to replace your belongings after a theft or disaster, you would need a renter's policy.

Health Insurance

Health-insurance rates are rising at a disproportionate rate. However, health insurance is something no one should be without. Nothing can be more financially devastating than a major medical event that has to be paid out of pocket. Every 30 seconds in the United States, someone files for bankruptcy in the aftermath of a serious health problem.[1]

Although the health-insurance landscape is rapidly changing, often the most cost-effective way to buy health insurance is through your employer. That is because an employer negotiates a group rate for all employees. Many times this group rate is significantly lower than an individual rate. Factors that determine the amount of your premium on an individual basis are your age, medical history, and physical condition.

It is important to note that dental and vision insurance are not typically included in a health-insurance policy. Coverage for these two components can often be added for an additional fee.

Buying Life Insurance: Know Your Mission

I think it is important to understand that, although insurance agents are often really great people, they are also in the business of selling insurance to make money. It is inevitable that some of them will try to sell you permanent insurance in situations where cheaper term life insurance might work better for you. Permanent insurance is made up of whole, variable, and universal, each of which have both a life-insurance component and an investment component combined. The investment

[1]David U. Himmelstein, Deborah Thorne, Elizabeth Warren, and Steffie Woolhandler, "Medical Bankruptcy in the US, 2007: Results of a National Study," *American Journal of Medicine* 122, no. 8 [August 2009]: 741–746.

component could be anything, from subaccounts that provide a contract rate, or that invest in bonds or stocks. Although a permanent life policy can build cash value that you can borrow against or draw from in the future, it's not without high internal expenses that you should consider carefully. Agents can make a commission 10 to 15 times greater on permanent life insurance than they do on term life insurance, so there is a big incentive for them to sell you on it. Do your homework and make sure it's right for you before you buy.

As a general rule, I would say that for most *Combat Finance* readers, it is better to buy less expensive term insurance and use the savings to increase your regular investments into your Roth, IRA, or 401(k). However, the key here is that you must be disciplined enough to consistently invest the amount you saved by going with term insurance. If you do that, and invest in a well-diversified and reasonably priced portfolio, you have a very strong chance of having your investments grow faster than they would have inside the insurance product. The fees on the investment portion of the permanent life policies are generally much higher than what you buy in a Roth, IRA, or other investment account. The investment choices inside the permanent life insurance product are also limited, whereas most Roth or IRA accounts at major brokerage firms have access to just about any stock, bond, mutual fund, or index fund. This gives you much more flexibility to choose an allocation that is right for you.

Like all rules of thumb there are exceptions, and one of the rare times a permanent life insurance policy makes sense is for the very wealthy—those whose wealth has grown beyond the current federal estate, gift, and goods and service tax exclusion limit of $5.25 million per person as of 2013—who will need to provide liquidity to their heirs to pay the estate taxes owed on an illiquid business or ranch. For this estate-planning situation, which we call "wealth replacement," we use permanent insurance. For most other instances, term insurance is a more appropriate and less expensive life insurance option.

"A" Way

Insurance can truly save someone's life in the case of a tragedy. One of my clients came to me years ago to consolidate all her family's financial endeavors with our company. We worked to consolidate a few of the husband's previous 401(k)s into one account, brought their investment accounts together, and looked at their college savings and retirement goals. One of the things we looked at during that consolidation was their insurance needs. She and her husband had four kids, and she was a stay-at-home mom. Although she did work from time to time, their saying was, "He puts the meat on the table and I put the flowers on," meaning they lived off his salary but her salary was for vacations and other wants. So when I started to look at what kind of insurance they had, I found that they only had her husband's policy through work, which paid two-times his annual salary in the case of his death. That simply wasn't enough to get four kids all the way through college and to cover all her living expenses in the event that he passed away. I started asking what they would want if he passed away. She said she wanted the house paid off so the kids could continue to grow up in the place they've known as their own. He said he wanted to have enough to pay for their college educations. She said she wanted to have enough to get her on her feet if he died or provide a big enough chunk that she could invest the remaining money and she could live off the income. So eventually we figured out that they needed much more life insurance than they had. And it's lucky that we figured it out when we did, because not more than a few months after accomplishing their insurance goal, he died of a heart attack and left behind his wife and four kids. It was really tragic and tough on this family, but it was one of those situations in which I can honestly say that their lives would be so massively different if they hadn't defended their home front so thoroughly before his death. Instead of struggling to make ends meet, as they would with the previous level of life insurance coverage that they had, all four kids have graduated college. They're doing great in their careers and moving on to new lives. This man was in his early fifties. No one would have ever thought that he'd be at risk. But sometimes things do happen, and we have to be realistic about the lifestyle we expect and how we're going to defend that if one of the income-generating members of the family passes away. In real life, sometimes the hero of the story does die or get injured or sick, and we've got to be able to recover from that, both financially and emotionally. Insurance helps you do that.

KEY TASK 1: Purchase disability insurance to replace a minimum of 60 percent of the gross income for all adult earners in the family.

This key task will allow us to prepare in the event that a breadwinner is permanently or temporarily injured or ill and unable to work. This could be a mental or physical illness or injury. It could be something that puts you out of work for months or years or possibly forever. It allows the time to heal and deal with the disability without the financial pressures that can compound this. This minimum of 60-percent of gross income replacement would allow the time you need—while still having to cut expenses—to get back on your feet as a family. Disability insurance is often overlooked, but it's so important. Imagine living the rest of your life seriously injured with only social security disability benefits. And even then, social security disability benefits aren't always available for everyone in all cases. Oftentimes the most cost-effective policies for disability insurance are offered through your employer, so check there as well as getting a quote from a few of your preferred agents. And don't forget that replacement for 60 percent of your gross income is a minimum. We use this in *Combat Finance* because it often provides adequate protection without the higher costs of larger percentages. But you should price out different plans to decide what is right for you. Anything less than 60 percent replacement is soup sandwich.

KEY TASK 2: Purchase a minimum of 10 times the annual household gross income in life insurance for the main breadwinner.

KEY TASK 3: Purchase a minimum of five times the annual household gross income in life insurance for the non-breadwinner.

Both of these key tasks are symbiotic. If someone in your household dies, life insurance is there to fund the funeral arrangements, take care of the family as you grieve the loss of a loved one, and to provide a possible nest egg that prevents a tragedy of that magnitude from derailing your financial goals such as college savings, home purchase, or retirement. Each year, Americans arrange more than 2 million funerals for family members and friends and they spend more than $6,000 on the traditional funeral, according to the Federal Trade Commission. Many funerals can run well over $10,000. That's money that already has a job, a purpose, in your *Combat Finance* battle plans. So planning for these events through life insurance not only makes you a defensive genius, it will give you the peace of mind you need to get through your day without worrying about what you would do if tragedy struck.

CPT Adair: The Fighting Adjutant

No one I know understands the defensive battle better than our Afghanistan-deployed squadron adjutant Captain Scott Adair. Adair coordinated our squadron's administrative services, acting as a human resources nerve center for all the things that come up in theatre, and all the things that come up back home when soldiers are serving overseas. He oversaw everything our soldiers went through during a difficult time in their lives, and he definitely saw when a family was prepared for problems and when a family wasn't. Adair could always tell which families were prepared, because they had communicated with their loved ones about what bad things could happen and what their families back home would experience in that case. They had set up plans for their family in the case of an injury or death. The families had basically run battle drills back home to deal with the eventualities of war, and the smart ones were financially prepared for it.

"People who were prepared discussed process," he says. "They understood what things would look and sound like if a soldier died, was injured, or something else happened. They knew that they didn't need to worry unless military personnel showed up at their door unannounced. They would have known that someone had died because that's the procedure in that case. I knew families weren't prepared if they panicked every time they saw news of military deaths in the media, because if they were prepared they would know that the Army would notify them well before the media of any casualty."

Adair knows that soldiers who were unprepared for injury or illness almost always pass the pain and suffering to their families. Soldiers are told over and over about the risks of war, and yet, just like regular civilians, they tell themselves that it could never happen to them. They don't update the beneficiary on their insurance, or they don't let anyone know their wishes for a funeral. And guess what? It's the family that has to deal with those problems after a loved one dies. It's the family that, in the middle of grieving a terrible loss, has to pinch pennies to make a funeral happen, or argue over what they think this person would have wanted because they don't know.

"I took out a life insurance policy for my newborn son after he was born and some people in my family were so upset," Adair says. "I think it's because it's so difficult and morbid to think about death before it happens. Why would I prepare for something so dark and so terrifying? It can be insulting, too, to feel as though there is a connection to someone's value in dollars. As though, if we do, it might have a greater chance of happening. But I've seen what happens after the death of a child. Like a bad horror movie, the family of the soldier is left wondering, where does the half million dollars go? It's amazing what happens. That policy was to protect my wife and me in case the unthinkable happened. That if we lost this precious part of our life, we wouldn't have to be squeezing nickels and dimes at a time when we would be devastated. That was worth $1 a month to me. Some people are superstitious, and that scares them, I guess, but I think of it as protection and defense in case I have to deal with the unthinkable."

It's about discussing, at length, a plan with a clear decision about what your family wants in the case of a death, even if it seems trivial at a time when everyone is healthy.

"It's right up there with getting that loose door handle fixed in the garage," says Adair. "We know it won't take long, but once we get started there are so many possibilities of other hassles or details that are connected to that. Getting prepared for the possibility of tragedy is like that. We need to take the time to look at our options even if it seems trivial or a hassle right now. We all know someone in our lives who passed away too soon, and sometimes they leave a mess of unanswered questions and financial problems in their wake as well."

By accomplishing your second and third key tasks in this chapter, you'll have answered those questions and prepared for the worst

The Fighting S-1
Captain Adair on patrol. Personnel and contracting tasks complete—Check. Get outside the wire whenever possible—Check.

to defend yourself in the case of that tragedy. There are many things to consider when determining what to buy, but at a minimum I want you to meet these key tasks.

KEY TASK 4: Establish a will or trust for all adult family members.

This task is another seemingly trivial step in the defensive part of protecting your home front. Without a will or trust, you have no idea what anyone in your family knows about your desires or plans, and vice versa. This step is about clarifying your financial choices, your personal choices for your funeral, and answering any lingering questions your family may have in case you unexpectedly die. Because in his job he deals with these issues all the time, Adair understands this implicitly.

After he came home from deployment he saw a weakness in his own family. His grandmother had three sons and a daughter, and she never discussed with any of them what she wanted when she dies.

"I've been to a few funerals on funeral details and I could see which of them went well and which didn't," Adair said. "I told my dad that grandma thinks she's going to live forever, which is great, but she's still got some assets, and she needs to make sure to put someone in charge to do the right things with those assets. To make sure everyone knows what she wants because she won't be there. Then when the whole thing does eventually happen, no one can say anything about the choices because she made it very clear in her will and through her trustee what it is she wants."

Adair said that he prompted his dad to have the conversation with his mother. They put together a clear plan and decided where everything would go when her time came. "It's almost like a research of death, it's so morbid," Adair said. "But it's a whole lot better than the alternative, which is complete chaos and people disagreeing and eventually hating each other because they all believe they know what their mother would have wanted. Before they discussed it with her, they all thought they knew what she wanted, but after the discussions they found out that they were mostly wrong."

KEY TASK 5: Evaluate long-term-care insurance for all adults aged 50 or older in the family.

In your final key task you need to look at what you would do if you had to defend against a long-term-care situation for someone in your family. This is generally something that you will want to start seriously evaluating for adults who are 50 or older, but even if you are not yet that experienced, keep reading so you'll know what to do when you are. Long-term-care insurance generally covers someone who has any number of diseases or illnesses that require skilled or nursing care from professionals for months or years—anything from Alzheimer's to MLS to cancers to a broken hip after a fall. When people need help bathing, dressing, using the toilet, transferring from a bed to a chair, taking care of incontinence or eating, they are in need of long-term care for activities of daily living. It's something that happens as we age. In the state of Nevada, for instance, these costs average about $5,000 per month. Someone can have a very considerable and comfortable retirement savings, but if one person in your family needs this type of care and someone isn't capable of giving it to them in the home, then it can drain all your retirement resources away.

Unfortunately, Medicaid doesn't kick in until most of your assets are wiped out. You would have to be down to just owning a primary residence, your personal belongings, and one car before Medicaid will help. In that case, there are no other assets to assist a spouse or provide income for him or her. Long-term-care insurance would assist them in covering the expenses related to one spouse requiring the services of a nursing home, while their retirement investments would continue to give the healthy spouse income to live on. Everyone should have a plan for this: either price out a long-term insurance policy or determine if you have a pension or other income that could cover those expenses. That way a healthy spouse doesn't face the prospect of a long healthy life in front of them with no assets or income as a result of their spouse's nursing-home expenses.

Combat Finance Professional Development (CFPD)

Combat Finance readers, welcome back to combat finance professional development training. We are going to broaden our experience this time by bringing in a naval officer to share his insights and experience. I have known Carl Fuetsch for just over 20 years now, ever since his son Curtis became one of my best friends in college and later the best man at my wedding. I have really enjoyed getting to know Carl over the last two decades and greatly admire him for many reasons, including his service, not just to our country but also to his community. He is very involved in charitable organizations throughout the Reno area, most notably the Reno Rotary Club where he currently serves as the club president. You are going to see from Carl that the road to success is not always linear because life throws in a few curve balls. But as a dear friend of mine is fond of saying, "Good people stay with good people," and I think you'll see that Carl had some good people working with him in the Navy, and they got him through some tough times. I hope you'll think about how you can be there for others as you read Carl's story. Let's take a look.

Name:	Carl T. Fuetsch, CDR, USN – Ret.
Total years of service:	27
Rank:	Commander, U.S. Navy, Retired
Combat Deployments:	
	Operation(s)
Cuba	1962, PHIBRON 6, USS Chilton (APA-38)
Vietnam	Multiple Deployments in Vietnam Waters 1967–1971 On both Yankee Station and Delta Station Operations Served variously on *Enterprise, Midway, Constellation*, and *Kitty Hawk* and detachment on other carriers and with Air Wings and Carrier Group staffs.
Nicosia, Cyprus	Emergency Military Evacuation Sept 1974 of U.S. Embassy due to murder of Ambassador Roger Davies and three other embassy staff members by Greek Cypriot militias.

KN: Carl, thank you so much for sharing your experiences over an impressive career with us. How old were you when you first began your military service?
CF: *17 years, 9 months.*

KN: Wow, you got started right away. Which branch did you enlist/commission into, and why did you choose that branch of service?
CF: *U.S.Naval Reserves and U.S. Navy—enlisted in April 1960—no choice in the matter; my father dragged me to the recruiter and signed me up as I was not meeting family academic expectations—I was having too much fun and skiing way too much. June 1960,*

the morning following high school graduation, I was on a bus to Recruit Training in San Diego. After release from active duty in July 1962 (served on USS Norton Sound *(AVM-1), Naval Academy Prep School (NAPS), Bainbridge, MD, and* USS Chilton *(APA-38), I still had a four-year commitment in the U.S. Naval Reserves while attending college. The Navy offered to pay my way through college if I would take a commission upon graduation. It was a good deal, so I joined the Reserve Officer Candidate (ROC) Program. The Vietnam conflict started while I was in college and the handwriting was on the wall—I'd get activated one way or another, and the choices were returning as an E-5 or E-6 or returning as a Commissioned Officer. I learned during my earlier active duty stint that being an Officer was much more interesting, and you got a stateroom with only 1 or 2 roommates rather than sleeping in a berthing compartment with 150 of your shipmates. Not only that, it provided far better opportunities in that it opened doors to additional responsibility and education. I returned to active duty in June, 1966 and remained on active duty for an additional 20+ years.*

KN: So you have experienced both boot camp and officer basic course. Would you describe some of your experiences?
CF: *Boot camp was a rather pleasant experience in learning and physical training. I had a great Chief Petty Officer as the Company Commander, and he made getting up at 0400 the best experience it could be—almost! It was very educational watching him mold 50 civilian kids into a cooperative, obedient, and somewhat educated team. Although almost everyone was going into different specialties, everyone had to learn the basics. You had to know how to keep the ship afloat, basic seamanship, gunnery, missiles, firearms, and so on. And you had to learn that everyone started at the bottom with KP, and you worked your way up by learning, cooperating, organizing, and getting the job done correctly. People who did not fit in or were incapable of integrating themselves into a unit were quickly removed or sent back to retraining. Boot camp was long enough to incentivize us not to get sent back twice on the way to goal line. The basic objective was to create team players who knew how to cooperate for designated goals and knew the basic terminology and practices. Boundaries were set on performance,*

standards explained and upheld, and expectations were always high and were regularly increased. All in all, it was a great team-building exercise. Financially, I was earning $48.00/month and was as rich as I could be—since there was no place to spend the money—so I started my first savings program because I could not spend all the money. Being somewhat lazy, I kept that same allotment in effect, increased by the same percentage as every pay raise for the next 27 years. That worked!

Part of the Navy's Reserve Officer Candidate (ROC) Program was attending the Navy Officer Candidate School (OCS) in Newport, Rhode Island, split into two 10-week summer sessions between your sophomore/junior and your junior/senior years of college. While back in the Reserve Unit, after your first summer at OCS, you were now a midshipman, wearing an officer's uniform with a junior officer responsibility of being a Division Officer. That responsibility was mind blowing for an enlisted E-5 now wearing a "strange" khaki uniform. You were now responsible for the performance of all the personnel, keeping their social life within acceptable bounds, all reporting, administration, promotions, Article 15's, and so forth, and of course their pay and allowances. It was a great, very quick, training in responsibility for life!

The next step, after graduation and commissioning, was Basic Aviation Officers Training at Pensacola. That, after boot camp, the ROC program, and OCS, I figured training at Pensacola would be a snap. Wrong! We did boot camp all over again, with PT, running, swimming, firefighting, shipboard emergencies, and so forth, because most of the individuals in the program had yet to go through the basics. Of course the Navy looked at everyone's records and appointed those of us with some background as Company Officers. It is really true that, by the third time you do something; you get rather efficient and effective. But a new wrinkle was thrown in—learning how to deal with difficult bosses and leaders. Oh, I forgot to mention, the Basic Aviation Officer Company Commanders were U.S. Marine Corps Gunnery Sergeants (Drill Sergeants)—that was an eye opener for a newly commissioned ensign of any stripe. Having been on active duty, progressing from E-1 to E-6 and getting commissioned, I thought I knew almost everything. Wrong! U.S. Marine Corps Gunnery Sergeants really taught me the importance of taking care of your "troops," full time, all the time, and all aspects of their lives, on duty or not! The language and phrases were colorful, pointed, efficient, and effective—and totally recallable although not particularly useable in civilian society.

KN: Well Carl, some great lessons to be learned there, and now I know where Curtis gets his vocabulary. Which values have you learned in the military that have made you a better employee or business person?

CF:

- *Chain of Command—There is always a boss that you will have to deal with, and you must get your job done whether you like it or not!*
- *Responsibility—Responsibility is doing the whole job! If you put your mind to it you can both do and enjoy almost any job. No job satisfaction results without completing the whole job.*
- *Planning—There is a process to success, and planning provides the steps that must be accomplished. Directly applicable in both military and civilian life. Keep focused on the objectives to achieve the objectives. It is way too easy to be diverted.*
- *Attitude matters—to both you (for your own job satisfaction) and to your organization (to complete the mission).*

KN: Responsibility, planning, attitude, and professionalism; great stuff, Carl. How has your military experience shaped your approach to your personal finances?

CF:

- *Recognition that finances are ALWAYS a major factor in both your professional life and personal life. You and your buddies all got paid and each of you was responsible for your own financial management, even though your monthly pay check (in 1960 dollars) was only $48. In our early years, occasionally we all blew our pay checks and were flat broke till the next payday—a great learning experience if you used it as a learning experience. We all know people that never related their current actions to their future needs. Those are the people that were never successful in the military or in life.*
- *In the military, both enlistees and officers had the opportunity to spend the government's money—which hopefully you realized were the taxes you paid out of your meager paycheck.*

- *In the military you were always a member of a team and responsible for your actions as well as inaction. Responsible to your superiors and responsible to your juniors. That exercise of responsibility extended to your family, and since finances are a critical part of having a successfully family, both while in the military and in later civilian life, you must pay attention to finances. Paying attention to finances will give you the time to pay attention to a career.*
- *In every case, if something is not planned and executed properly, it will fail or end up as the lowest common denominator solution that comes with a guarantee that you won't like the result!*

KN: Choices have consequences. That is such a valid lesson in every area of our lives. Tell us about the proudest moment of your military career and how you think it has affected you as an employee or business person.
CF: *The proudest moments have always been related to having and completing a successful tour of duty related to being in charge, be it a Division Officer tour with 30 people, an Operations tour with multiple Divisions, a command tour of a small, medium, or large organization. The size of the organization is not necessarily the driver of proudest moments. Those moments are created by the difficulty of turning a group of people into a great functioning, integrated body that is recognized by everyone as great. That is the satisfaction that makes you proud. A challenging job, well done and recognized.*

KN: It sounds like you experienced some great teamwork and camaraderie during your time in service. If you would, please tell us about the most difficult moment or experience in your military career and how you think it affected you as an employee or business person.
CF: *This story shows how life can go to hell and how support from great Navy seniors saved the situation and kept a career on track. As a very junior Navy LT with only three years' commissioned experience, I received a wonderful set of orders, well above my rank, to be the Assistant Intelligence Officer on the USS* Enterprise *(CVAN-65), in the middle of the Vietnam War. It was a position usually assigned to a seasoned Lieutenant Commander. I had great expectations of running*

all the intelligence computers and communications systems on that great carrier and being the deputy to the best and the brightest fast-track Navy Commander who had been assigned as the Enterprise's *Senior Intelligence Officer. Of course, that required schooling, and, of course, the school was on the opposite coast of the country. In the Volkswagen Beetle, with my newly pregnant wife and family dachshund, we were off on a new adventure. We got to the training site at a newly commissioned Naval Air Station (NAS Albany), Georgia (former Turner Air Force Base), found temporary housing, and came to an agreement with the wife over use of the VW, when my wife complained about an itching mole on her back. Not being too concerned, she made an appointment at the NAS Dispensary for a quick look-see by the local flight surgeon. After about four weeks of waiting for analysis of the mole, the flight surgeon called us both into his office and broke the news that my now five-month-pregnant wife had malignant melanoma and had, at the most, one year to live. Our world blew up! The flight surgeon immediately notified the commander of the school, a Navy Captain who dropped everything and came to the dispensary with his wife to gather us up. We were made comfortable, counseled, taken care of, and prepared for future eventualities. In civilian life, this is called a support system; the military recognized the need and had the system established and operational at a moment's notice with experts available for every eventuality. After several days, we decided that I would continue through the school, graduate, and proceed to the USS* Enterprise. *The Big "E" had just finished nuclear refueling in Newport News, VA, so I immediately flew up and reported in. The Commanding Officer of the* Enterprise, *the Operations boss and 'ship's Intelligence Officer met me and made arrangements to check me aboard and fly me back to my wife at NAS Albany as soon as possible in the ship's aircraft. The ship was getting ready to change homeports from Newport News Shipyard in Virginia to NAS Alameda, California, by going around the Horn to the Pacific. As I had already reported aboard, I was now assigned to the USS* Enterprise *and would meet the ship after graduation from school. School was expedited, and the Navy picked up all our personal belongings, flew my wife to her family in Reno to await the ship's arrival in Alameda. As can be imagined, at that point in time, our world was in chaos, our thinking and planning was at low ebb, what with a pregnancy, cancer, a coast-to-coast move with household goods, ship and homeport movement, and so on.*

The Navy command structure jumped into the void and did everything possible to keep us on track, facilitating appropriate medical trips to medical specialists in New Orleans, Pensacola, Bethesda, and so on. The total support package continued to support us. My wife did die a year and a day after diagnosis, and again the Navy jumped into the breach moving me ashore, assigning me to a great position with on-base housing as well as a challenging position. What were the take-aways? Number one is that planning works! If you want a successful life, you need to plan all the contingencies, not just the fun or easy ones. If and when you get into business, own a business, or run a large operation, your assets are not your money—they are the people! Take care of them, and they will take care of you. Money (salary) flows from your performance of your job, and it will come if you become a "servant"! What do I mean by that? It's doing the job focusing on the employees and people you work with; planning for their benefit and profit gets the job done. When that happens, everyone gains.

KN: Carl, I can't thank you enough for sharing that story with us. The Navy was a great family for you in your time of need, and you, in turn, served dutifully and selflessly as well. I loved your closing emphasis on planning and people. Those are great lessons.

Taking on a lighter tone, what was the funniest or most embarrassing moment of your military career? What did you learn from that experience?

CF: *I have always had funny and embarrassing moments in my career. In fact, funny and embarrassing moments have been the highlight of my 27 years of service. What you probably don't know is that funny and embarrassing moments are great opportunities to raise the spirit and moral of the organization by turning those funny and embarrassing moments into something positive and uplifting. Turn it into legend in the organization by owning up to the event and making it a lesson of what to do or not to do. Most people remember lessons associated with something uplifting rather than with doom and gloom. The best commanders I've worked for all had this knack and used it to the organization's benefit.*

One of the most significant embarrassing moments I was involved in started out toward being a major disaster for the U.S. Navy. But, due to a strong, morally based, proactive series of decisions by the Captain, it became an example of how to overcome one of the greatest sins a Naval Officer could commit. The "sin" was running the USS Enterprise *(CVN-65) aground in San Francisco Bay as we returned from a seven-month deployment to the Pacific, Indian Ocean, and North Arabian Sea. We were within sight of the Carrier Piers at Alameda, California, when we lost all power and an incoming tide pushed us up against the south edge of the dredged channel to Alameda Naval Air Station. We were dead in the water with thousands of dependents standing on the pier about a mile away. As is well known, running carriers (or any ship) aground is not conducive to a long career. In Navy tradition running your ship aground is always the captain's fault, but in this case what the captain did after the ship ran aground saved his career.*

My part in this event is tangential. As a Staff Officer ('Assistant Chief of Staff —Intelligence) on Carrier Group Three aboard the Enterprise *we were of little use to the ship, so Carrier Group Three staff officers were assigned as escort officers for all the VIPs riding the ship back into port. My assignment was to escort Mayor Dianne Feinstein around the ship, keep her informed of events, and explain and answer her questions. Yes, she had a* lot *of questions!*

The Captain immediately announced what happened to all hands (as if it was not kind of obvious). All the mayors, congressmen, and such from the Bay Area were aboard (including Mayor Diane Feinstein, Congressman Dellums, and others), and they were kept abreast of the status of the event. The Captain paid attention to the details and relayed them all to his crew and visitors. The Captain called the Commander Naval Air Forces Pacific (Vice Admiral) in San Diego and personally updated him and asked that he come up to Alameda immediately. (He was aboard the Enterprise *in less than 90 minutes—it helps to have your own jet.) The* Enterprise's *Captain did everything right; he kept his crew informed, kept the politicians satisfied, took their questions, assigned people to follow up, flew the VIPs off the ship so they could make their meetings, notified all the correct people, and most importantly immediately accepted blame. At the same time, he presented the plan to recover from the grounding. As soon as the tide turned, the tugs pushed us back in the channel, and we proceeded to the Carrier Piers and tied up. Very little damage to the ship, lots of pissed off dependents that waited seven hours on the pier for us to cover the last mile home from deployment. The Captain, probably the finest Navy Captain I ever knew, went on to Command the Pacific Fleet as a four-star Admiral.*

Carl, that was absolutely outstanding. Thank you for taking the time to share so many great life lessons that we can apply to our careers, our businesses, our families, and our finances. It just goes to show that not all career and educational paths are linear, but if you do the right things for the right reasons and always strive for improvement, the general direction is up. Congratulations on a fine career and thank you so much for your service to the United States Navy and our nation.

Combat Finance readers, you can look forward to more combat finance professional development (CFPD) as you move to the next chapters.

Do Your Heirs Know Your Last Wishes?

People underestimate how devastating disasters can be. If you have an emergency and you don't have insurance, you could be forced to wipe out your investments. After all, it seems emergencies never happen when the market is up and the economy is great. So to properly defend our home front from tragedy and disaster, *Combat Finance* readers have to act defensively for possible future attacks on our family's and our own happiness and well-being. As someone who conducted military funerals on funeral detail, Adair has a unique perspective on death and preparing for the worst-case scenario. He sees it as a mentally demanding task.

"We conduct final honors for our veterans and fellow soldiers all the time. It's actually pretty common," he says. "But I learned after the first couple months that there was nothing routine or common in the emotions that soldiers, family, or friends have at these services. There is no uniformity in the emotional reaction we have to death. Death is something that no one should have to think about, but we have to think about it at least once per year when we sit down and fill out our employee benefits election or military insurance forms. I know it's a blessing to have these at all, but it's still awkward to talk about death in a routine way. I've seen that when we lay soldiers to rest. At the funerals of those soldiers who communicated what they wanted early and clearly, there was a sense of calm understanding, of happiness even, in the air because the service could happen without distraction. No one had to second guess what this person wanted. The families are thanking the person who died for not completely abandoning them, for providing guidance and direction while they're in such a dark place grieving this loss. That's why we prepare for death; not for ourselves, but for the well-being of our families."

The military is not made up of individual heroes who do things on their own. This chapter should hit that home because, let's face it, the Coast Guard doesn't get the attention that the other services do. People don't talk at dinner parties about their cousin in the Coast Guard, right? Instead, everyone has a cousin who is a Navy SEAL, or a fighter pilot, or a marine on the front lines. In many ways, that's not fair. If we all thought about what the Coast Guard provides to us on the home front, we'd recognize their vital role in protecting our security is every bit as necessary and heroic as that Navy SEAL on a top-secret mission. Insurance is the Coast Guard of finance. It doesn't get nearly the attention it should for its important role in protecting our operations at home. It's underappreciated in so many ways, but a critical piece of our financial security.

After Action Review

If you have finished this chapter successfully and have completed the following tasks, you are hereby promoted to Sergeant First Class E-7 (SFC) in *Combat Finance*. You have:

1. Completed and maintained all key tasks from previous chapters.
2. Consistently followed your Combat Finance general orders.
3. Consistently maintained your financial bearing.
4. Completed your consumer debt pay-off plan from Chapter 1 and remained debt free.

5. Calculated and built your reserves as described in Chapter 2.
6. Used the battlefield calculus described in Chapter 3 to budget for, save for, and purchase a home that you can defend in the face of financial attacks.
7. Established retirement savings of at least 10 percent of your income and made it automatic through payroll deduction or an automated weekly or monthly bank transfer.
8. Analyzed your insurance needs and at an absolute minimum:
   a. Purchased disability insurance to replace a minimum of 60 percent of the gross income for all adult earners in the family.
   b. Purchased a minimum of 10 times the annual household gross income in life insurance for the main breadwinner.
   c. Purchased a minimum of five times the annual household gross income in life insurance for the non-breadwinner.
   d. Established a will or trust for all adult family members.
   e. Evaluated long-term-care insurance for all adults in the family.

If you have not completed each of the key tasks in this chapter, *continue reading,* but you are barred from promotion until you meet these minimum standards.

By virtue of your promotion to *Combat Finance* Sergeant First Class, you are now a senior noncommissioned officer and as such you have taken on a greater responsibility for those around you. It is not by chance that this rank was chosen for this chapter. It is because a Sergeant First Class in the Army is traditionally a platoon sergeant with 15 to 40 soldiers counting on him or her, depending on the type of unit. It is the rank at which a noncommissioned officer (NCO) must shift from focusing on his or her own operational productivity toward that of supporting the success of the entire unit. A Sergeant First Class has soldiers and junior NCOs depending on him or her. In our financial lives, the need for wills and insurance become most apparent when we begin to have loved ones in our lives that depend on us.

Chapter 6

The Value of Advice

There's this type of bread in Afghanistan called dodday, and it's a flatbread that looks like an American pizza crust with no toppings. It's used in most meals there, especially to scoop up rice or other foods since most people don't use forks or knives, at least in the area where we were deployed. At one point during our deployment we had a Brigadier General visiting Mehtar Lam. He was the commander of the Nevada Air Guard at the time, and we took him out into the city on a patrol. During that patrol, one of our sergeants went over to a bread vendor and bought five pieces of dodday for $5. He was happy because it seemed like a great deal. He was busy handing pieces out to others and generally enjoying his score. Our interpreter, Aimal Halim, was watching all of this and strolled over to the sergeant to ask for $2. We all watched while Aimal went over and bought 20 pieces of dodday and brought them over to us. Instead of the $1 per piece that our sergeant paid, Aimal walked away with 20 pieces of bread for 10 cents each.

That sergeant was a very smart and capable soldier, and we all thought that he got a great deal, but this story is an example of how we don't really know what we don't know. That's true in so much of our lives. People make decisions every day, especially regarding their finances, without realizing that they don't have all the information at hand that an expert on the subject might. People do investment allocations on their own, they buy whole life insurance without consulting their financial advisor or CPA, they barter in stocks whose operations they don't fully understand. All these things, they believe, are the best decisions that they can make with the information they have on hand. These are intelligent people who are doing their best, and yet they don't have the experience to understand when they may not have a complete picture of the investment opportunity. It's a combination of knowledge and experience that ensures you don't pay $5 for five pieces of dodday when you could have had 20 pieces for $2.

Seek Wisdom, Avoid Overconfidence

How do we ensure that kind of knowledge and experience? By employing and engaging experts in every important part of our lives. These experts—anyone from doctors to attorneys to accountants to financial advisors and beyond—advise us about courses of action by using information that we might not have on hand and experience that they've gained in the field over many years. In an age when we have so much questionable information available to us via the Web, ensuring that any of us can access endless testimony about financial matters, it's important to understand that it's just as easy for us to become overconfident. There's this phenomenon noted in psychological research called illusory superiority, which is a human perception that causes people to overestimate their abilities and positive qualities, while underestimating their negative qualities in anything from intelligence to academic performance to athletic faculties. In a 1981 experiment, a Swedish psychologist named Ola Svenson surveyed hundreds of American and European students, asking them to compare their driving skills to the skills of others. More than 90 percent of the Americans surveyed in the study placed themselves in the top half of the population in driving skill. So basically, nearly all of us believe that we are great drivers, which is statistically impossible, of course. Another study done in the

Journal of Finance in 2002 looked at personal investment strategies and it found similar results: We are overconfident, and that can negatively affect our financial performance. Most people mentally count their winners and discount their losers. Successful investors and advisors take the illusory superiority bias out of the picture and look at returns objectively. They do this by comparing their portfolio returns with an appropriate benchmark, making sure to also compare things like standard deviation and capture ratios. If we all think we're great investors, that means that a lot of us haven't taken the time to truly measure our risk-adjusted returns and compare them to similar allocations as an expert would.

COL Mohammad Jan

One of the toughest and most competent officers I have met. He definitely knew what we did not know about Afghanistan.

Experts in finance know that most investment categories will eventually gravitate back to their mean long-term returns, and they can help you plan accordingly. Some examples of market corrections date all the way back to the 1600s. In the 1630s, a tulip-bulb scarcity pushed the price of one tulip to the cost of nearly an entire estate. Of course, the prices weren't an accurate reflection of the value of a tulip bulb, and they fell back down to the price of a common onion after a few years. You can see these same types of boom and bust corrections, on a different scale, in the oil and gas boom in the 1970s and the dot-com bubble in the late 1990s. Experience tells us that we have had cycles similar to this over time, and having experts who can keep us from getting caught up in the hype du jour may help us avoid big mistakes.

Experience combined with knowledge can produce wisdom, but it's important to understand that it does not automatically do so. You could have someone who reads everything there is to read, and he still may not be wise if he has no personal experience. You could have an army recruit who has the soldier's handbook by his side 24/7. He could read through every word, every chapter, and still not fully grasp what a combat engagement is like because he doesn't have the experience to understand. When I was a new soldier, our unit was mechanized infantry, but often we conducted our training dismounted. On one of my first drill weekends we were patrolling through the Nevada sagebrush. Our mission was to go down and clear a draw that sat below a small hill. It was a simple operation order that had been given, but in hindsight, it was a little too simple. We started the patrol at night, and since it was 1990, we didn't have night vision goggles, so we fanned out and did our best to move quietly through the sagebrush. Over to our side someone started to shoot at us so our squad leader had us bound toward the enemy since it looked like only two rifle flashes against the eight or nine of us in our squad. When we got closer, though, the entire hillside lit up. They had set us up for an ambush and had shot at us to get us to come over. Thank goodness we train with blank ammunition.

Looking back with the experience I have now, I realize that it was stupid for us to run into that. It seemed like a great idea at the time because none of us were experienced enough to understand what we didn't know. I learned so much from that. I learned not to rush into things. And I learned that in that situation I needed to utilize an expert leader to help us feel comfortable in stopping, going to ground, assessing the situation, and then acting. You couldn't read any of that in a soldier's handbook because we only gain it from experience. It's the same with our finances. There are so many self-help financial firms out there that make it seem so easy to do, but you don't have the experience to know what you don't know and that can be dangerous. Professionals not only have time under their belt (if you choose the right one), but they learn from the experience of all their clients over the years. They have seen what works and what doesn't. Don't get lured into a sense of security just because you have a breadth of knowledge at your disposal. You need experts with experience and knowledge and a track record of demonstrating wisdom.

Selecting Your Cabinet

Even our best presidents need an extraordinary cabinet of experts with decades of experience to help them through a successful presidency. For the sake of this book, we're going to use a comparison to the President of the United States and his (someday her) cabinet or administration to explain the structure that you must build in your household in this chapter. That doesn't mean that you've been promoted to commander-in-chief already (you'll be promoted on schedule at the end of the chapter if you complete your key tasks), but it's a useful and easily understood way of illustrating the structures of your household. You're now the president of your own financial plan, of your own financial country. Actually, it's probably your spouse who is in charge if we're being completely honest, but you're definitely at least the vice president. You and your spouse and family have to make decisions about how you're going to spend your budget. You have to be able to make that budget work, which means that you have to decide when and how much you're going to take out of your resources to put toward things like leisure and luxury. Your budget, just like your FOB, needs to be defendable. If you take too much of your generated income or your resources to put toward wants, like expensive cars, homes, and vacations, then you won't have enough resources to create growth. We want to maintain an adequate growth trajectory in your own financial nation by making choices that will lead to a rich lifestyle later, such as funding our 401(k) and investing for our children's education.

In the course of doing this, you will be under constant pressure from the lobbyists out there trying to get you to spend more and more on your wants and those of your family. The ironic thing is that the most powerful lobbyists out there are you, your family, and your friends. There are other lobbyists out there too, like advertisements and magazines, and it's tough to fight them, so your budget is an absolutely critical line of defense to help keep you on track. Your spouse may want a vacation, and you may want to get some new furniture, and your 16-year-old may want a new car, but those expenses are wants, and they will not lead to greater productivity or wealth later on. That's not to say that you can't do these things; it just means that you have to prioritize and make sure you can do the most important things first and still afford to add in the wants. If you have a detailed budget, you can blame the budget and let it be the bad guy when you have to say no to the lobbyists. It takes the political pressure off you.

Just as the President must set his priorities, you must sit down with your family to determine your strategic objectives. Once you have done that, you must clearly articulate those objectives to your cabinet, and they will help you apply your resources to meet those goals. Because this is such an important process, it is critical that you choose your cabinet wisely so that you trust them to manage the issues within their control. If you find yourself micromanaging issues that should be handled by your cabinet, the problem is you. You either need to back off and let them do their job, or you need to do a better job of selecting, communicating with, and supervising your administration. Remember, you preside over your financial country, but your cabinet runs it.

Since your administration exists to help you achieve your strategic objectives, you must have four primary cabinet members. They include an experienced financial advisor, a skilled attorney, a competent CPA, and an insurance agent who has your interests in mind. This cabinet will help you achieve your overall strategic objectives for retirement, college expenses, vacations, travel, hobbies, vehicles, and other goals.

It's important to note that you need to pick outstanding individuals to advise you in your cabinet. So how do you do that? First, be aware that just because a great number of experts have the same title doesn't mean they're all alike. There are good and bad accountants, even if they all have a CPA title, just as there are good and bad officers and NCOs, even if they all share the same title. The people you choose need to

Major Lau and "Red" Najib
If I'm putting together a team, my first pick is Major Lau. His competence, character,and work ethic are second to none. Build your cabinet with people who share these qualities and compliment your strengths rather than duplicate them.

have a servant's heart and understand that your success is dependent not just on making you happy in the short run, but in helping you make the right choices for your financial future. In other words, many advisors will tell you what you want to hear in order to stay in your good graces, but a good advisor will tell you what you don't want to hear. I like to say that if you and your advisor always agree, then one of you is redundant. You want advisors who are knowledgeable, experienced, and wise in the ways of their profession. But most of all, you want advisors who are truthful even when the truth might make you want to leave them as a client. Note that impressive titles and designations are important, but trust, reputation, and integrity are just as important in these selections. See Table 6.1 for a list of the key cabinet positions you are going to select later in this chapter.

Table 6.1 Cabinet Positions

Cabinet	Name	Phone
Secretary of Defense		
Financial Advisor		
Secretary of State		
Attorney		
Treasury Secretary		
CPA		
Director of Homeland Security		
Insurance Agent		

In addition to your cabinet, albeit in a slightly less-crucial role, you'll also have a field of czars in your life who provide expert advice in areas that save you time. In the United States, we refer to high-level officials who oversee a particular policy as czars. You'll have a health-care czar (your doctor or dentist) who keeps you healthy and understands your medical history. You'll have a housing czar (your real-estate agent) who helps you select the housing you need. You'll have a loan czar (your mortgage broker) who will assist you in financing any real estate purchases. And you'll have a laundry list of other czars for pet care, house cleaning, hair styling, floral arranging, and other policy oversight. See Table 6.2 for some examples of the czars that you might need. Know and cultivate your czars as key participants in your financial and personal success. I save time every visit to my selected barber (my beauty czar) because he knows exactly what to do. I don't have to spend time explaining the standard operating procedures for this every time I go in, and I don't have to pay extra for someone else to do it. It's done right every time. I save time and get a better product when I go to my selected florist (my flower czar) because she knows exactly what types of flowers and colors my wife likes and is able to put together an arrangement that is beautiful without a ton of work from me.

My housing czar, who also happens to be my sister, has been key to my financial success. When we went to purchase a condo in Reno, the sellers wanted a lot of money in a down market. I did what I thought was a decent amount of research on the property and wanted to offer nearly $175,000 less than their asking price. It seemed like a great deal

Table 6.2 Czar Positions

Czar	Name	Phone
Mortgage broker		
Realtor		
Doctor		
Dentist		
Fitness (trainer)		
Veterinarian		
Housekeeper		
Landscaper		
Florist		

to me, and I even felt a little guilty for suggesting such a lowball offer. But my sister looked at the recent sales, prices per square foot in the area, the length of time it was on the market, how many loans they had against it, and how much they were paying on it in assessments, taxes, and interest payments while it was on the market. She saw that it was worth even less than what I thought. Her due diligence and experience saved us an additional $75,000. In that instance, I didn't know what I didn't know. She did, and she saved us a bundle.

Czars can be key to your success, but they are also secondary to your cabinet, which manages the most important missions in your financial life. To build your administration, you have to start with the key piece of your financial cabinet, your secretary of defense.

KEY TASK 1: Select a secretary of defense, your primary financial advisor.

Let's start with your secretary of defense, a position that used to be called the secretary of war. I point this out because this role is actually an offensive one in the scheme of your financial armed forces. This person is going to focus on your offensive operations by designing armed forces that work toward accomplishing each of your strategic objectives. Your secretary of defense is also going to work very closely with your other cabinet members.

The Secretary of Defense in the United States not only oversees the Joint Chiefs of Staff, which includes the head of the army, navy, air force, and marines, but he is also very involved in procuring resources for the defense department. He must be in tune with the strategic objectives of the President and work hand-in-hand with the Secretary of State, who is given the same strategic objectives, but works at them from a diplomatic approach. If the secretary of defense and the other members of your cabinet are not working toward the same objectives, it costs the country money and time in wasted effort. It can even be counterproductive.

Choosing the right candidate is very important, and even though we will talk about turning your strategic objectives into mission statements in detail in the next chapter, you will need to have a good idea of what your primary objectives will be in order to select the right advisor. Financial advisors have many different degrees of training, background, and experience, and they all approach financial solutions from a different perspective. These professionals can be called anything from financial planners to wealth managers to financial analysts. But these labels are somewhat generic, and you'll need to ask specifically how they will manage money for you. Credentials are important, but don't get caught up in designations beside someone's name as the only thing that matters. Check their record on the Financial Industry Regulatory Authority website to understand their background, training, education, disciplinary history, and income sources. Advisors who earn fees from clients must also register with the Securities and Exchange Commission or the comparable agency in the state where they practice. Search for the advisor on the SEC website to see if there is a history of repeated and troubling complaints. Understand what minimum amount of assets the advisor will work with and, above all, conduct an interview with the advisor to ask about their background, investing philosophy, risk approach, and fee schedule.

I believe that it is important to look at what the person does outside the office and their experience prior to becoming an advisor. Just as with anyone working for you, a solid track record of employment is a good sign, but a change in jobs or careers or even firms every few years is a red flag. You want someone who is passionate about finance and will be there to grow with you. You can tell a lot about someone by what they do outside the office, so take the time to do an internet search on your candidates to see who they are when they leave work. Does the image that develops match your values? You are going to go through some great times and some bad times with this person, like a marriage, so you want it to be someone you can work with. Finally, does this person work as part of a team and have a process? This person should be able to articulate exactly who does what on the team and be able to outline the process. Ask your most successful friends or relatives who they use. That will give you a list of names to start with. Don't ask your broke buddy or high-spending uncle. You want a professional who works with those who have money or who demonstrate that they are dedicated and disciplined enough to be on the path toward accumulating it. Remember, true professionals are just as diligent about whom they work with as you need to be. So if they are willing to work with your high spending uncle or your broke buddy they are not disciplined enough to work with a *Combat Finance* reader like you.

KEY TASK 2: Select your secretary of state, your attorney.

You may be asking why your attorney wouldn't be the attorney general. Well, we're using this analogy to teach a point here, so lighten up a bit and have some fun. Enjoy the ride. When it comes to your secretary of state, this person handles all the diplomacy for you. For example, while the military is handling combat operations in Afghanistan, the Secretary of State works to further our country's political objectives both within Afghanistan as well as in the surrounding countries like Pakistan and Iran. The Secretary of State has to work closely with the military to make sure their efforts are synchronized. She organizes and supervises the entire U.S. Department of State and the U.S. Foreign Service. She advises the President on all matters of foreign policy, including the appointment of diplomatic representatives to other nations and from other nations. She negotiates with other countries and is responsible for the overall direction, coordination, and supervision of government activities overseas. She also advises on travel, immigration policy, and communication issues.

If the Secretary of State were working counter to other members of the cabinet, that would be highly unproductive. Your attorney also works on many fronts. One way that he can do this is by managing an estate plan. For example, if a family wants to gift assets to their children over time in order to stay under estate tax limits and to avoid a heavy tax upon the death of the parents, a good financial advisor and attorney team will help them do that by working together, not counter to each other. They will also bring in the CPA and the insurance agent to assist in managing all related issues to maximize the benefit of the estate plan.

Who is your attorney? You should choose someone who is smart and experienced, and who demonstrates wisdom and sound judgment. Once again, ask people you admire and respect whom they use and why. That will give you a short list to work with. But remember, your first need is probably going to be a will or trust, so find an attorney who has experience in those matters, but also someone you can go to for advice on real estate questions, a dispute with neighbors, or other general issues from time to time. It has to be someone you're comfortable working with over the long run: someone honest, thorough, and responsive, within your price range, experienced, and working within a firm that is the right size. You might think that you don't need a secretary of state now, but if you follow my *Combat Finance* principles, you will eventually have wealth, and wealthy people need a good attorney.

KEY TASK 3: Select your treasury secretary, your CPA.

Another element of your cabinet is your secretary of the treasury, who monitors your tax compliance. The Secretary of the Treasury of the United States monitors monetary matters and plays a critical role in policy making by marrying governmental fiscal policy with economic development. In your household, this person will work closely with your financial advisor to ensure that your portfolio is optimized to take advantage of tax code while maximizing total return. Your secretary of the treasury will assist you with buying, managing, and exchanging certain real estate or business assets to manage things like expenses, depreciation, and capital gains. However, there is a reason the United

States has not combined the secretaries of the treasury and defense into one job, so don't do that with yours either. A CPA should focus on accounting, audits, and taxes because there is no way to do all of that professionally and still monitor investment portfolios each day as a good financial advisor does.

Your treasury secretary should always be a certified public accountant and not simply a registered agent or tax preparer. Anyone can be a registered agent—it only takes a minimal amount of studying and a short registration process—but a CPA's background means that she has gone through a myriad of checkpoints to get her license. Those requirements can include a bachelor's degree, nearly 50 semester hours of work in accounting and business, passing the Uniform CPA exam, passing an ethics course, and one year of general accounting experience supervised by a CPA with an active license. In many states the requirements are even more stringent. That's the kind of person you want on your cabinet. That's why there are fewer CPAs out there than there are bookkeepers, registered agents, or tax preparers. Being a licensed CPA imposes the burden of legal obligations, continuing education, and possible jail time if you mess up. CPAs may cost more for their time, but their time is much more valuable than someone who isn't licensed. Remember, price and value are different. As a *Combat Finance* reader, I want you to focus on value.

KEY TASK 4: Select your director of homeland security, your insurance agent.

The final element of your cabinet is your director of homeland security, who is your insurance agent. This person needs to work closely with the cabinet to ensure that all your assets are properly protected. The U.S. Secretary of Homeland Security is the head of the body that is concerned with protecting our home turf and the safety of American citizens. This position oversees the Coast Guard, the Federal Protective Service, the Border Patrol, the Secret Service, and the Federal Emergency Management Agency. This position must always focus on the defense of the home front. This is never an offensive position because offense is outside the area of that person's strengths and expertise. This cabinet member defends all the hard-earned wealth that you've developed by carefully assessing your needs, building a defense system, and evaluating it at regular intervals through thorough communication with your other cabinet members.

KEY TASK 5: Clearly communicate strategic objectives to the selected cabinet secretaries.

Once you have chosen your strategic objectives and selected your cabinet secretaries, you'll need to work with each secretary to ensure that they're operating toward the same goal. This is called unity of effort: the state of harmonizing efforts among multiple organizations working toward a similar objective. Communication is essential here for them to understand your purpose, key tasks, and end state. We will discuss these terms and show you how to write your mission statements in the next chapter, so for now, just understand that effective communication will allow you to develop and synchronize your plan for allocating resources to each of your cabinet departments. As always, you will have to ensure that you've met all *Combat Finance* minimums we discussed earlier in the book. But most importantly, know that communication with your cabinet is not a one-time event. It is necessary to reassess your situation and develop a current operating picture with these secretaries at least once per year. That kind of review will assure that the entire administration not only starts out on the right track, but stays on track even in the face of life's ever-present changes.

There is also a set of responsibilities for both you and the experts. Experts have the responsibility to give you the best possible advice. You have the responsibility to supervise, delegate, and oversee what they do. If you don't take this responsibility seriously, you can end up with a Bernie Madoff situation in which you are too trusting. Don't just say, "I don't know anything about this, just do it for me," because that can be more dangerous than just doing it yourself. Find a balance between seeking out others' advice, and still doing enough to hold them accountable. Delegate where you have to, then check their performance against your mission statements, and take corrective action when you need to.

There are many examples of how that kind of communication of your strategic objectives can save money. For example, for people who have an operational reserve, an established strategic reserve, and tactical reserves built into their investment accounts, it can be essential to consult with your insurance agent to address your coverage. For instance, if you were a college student when you signed up for your automobile coverage you may have gone with a higher monthly premium so that a large deductible didn't wipe you out. But now that you have reserves, you really only need your insurance to kick in if something really big happens. So you may want to work with your agent to find a policy with a smaller monthly cost and a larger deductible if something happened. If your insurance agent is in regular communication with you and your financial advisor, he or she will be able to save you money by properly assessing your needs as they change. The point is that the more your cabinet works together, the more opportunities you have to save. All of these efforts tie in together.

Combat Finance Professional Development (CFPD)

Combat Finance readers, welcome back to combat finance professional development training. Today we are going to hear from retired Colonel Steve Spitze. Steve was the commander of my unit, 1-221 Cavalry back when I was one of the troop commanders working for him. I have had the honor of working for some great officers in my 23 years, but Steve was one of the best. There were many leadership qualities that I admired about Steve, but two things really stood out. First was that he was extremely effective at balancing mission accomplishment with soldier care. Under his leadership our squadron met and surpassed every task we were assigned, but at the same time we had fun and never worked just to work. He set the objective, laid out how we were going to get there, and let us execute the plan. He stayed engaged with what was going on and if we were going off course or behind on schedule, he would provide guidance as needed, but I never felt like he was trying to run my troop. *I* got to run my troop as long as I was meeting *his* objectives. Second, Steve was one of the most intelligent officers I have worked with, and he always had a plan for his future. He rocketed up the ranks and became the chief of staff of the Nevada Army National Guard and made full colonel by his mid-30s. He then went to law school, came back to Nevada, and now holds an executive position with one of the world's largest gold-mining companies. As I said, he's a smart guy, so let's take a look at what he has to share with us.

Name: Steve Spitze, Colonel, U.S. Army—Retired
Total years of service: 20

KN: How old were you when you first began your military service?
SS: *18. I entered ROTC at the University of Nevada.*

KN: Nevada, now that's a great school. (Remember, warriors never hide their colors.) Which branch did you commission into and why did you choose that branch of service?
SS: *Army, because I preferred the ground aspects of the army's operations over the sea/air aspects of the navy/marines and air force.*

KN: Thinking back to Officer Basic Course or other training, describe some of your experiences. Did your TAC officer have certain phrases that he/she used or ways to "modify" your behavior that you distinctly remember as funny or creative . . . at least in hindsight?
SS: *Ranger School: hand-to-hand combat. The Ranger Instructor said, "Now, Rangers, when you are about to get in a fight, you should sound off with a thunderous 'HUAAAAAAH!'— this will give you that slight psychological edge." Now, this may not sound too funny, but picture a big, scary Ranger Instructor with a strong Southern accent and slight lisp—which really came out when he said, "ssslight psssychological edge." It was all we could do to not laugh at him; he probably would have killed us with his bare hands.*

KN: That sounds pretty funny, but I'm glad you kept your cool. Are there any values that you have learned in the military that have made you a better employee or business person?
SS: *Duty/work ethic. When you are given a job, you are expected to complete it—right and on time; no excuses. So you must know your job (what you are responsible for doing), know how to complete the job well, and complete it correctly and on time. In the military, your buddies, your unit, and your country depend on you. In the business*

world, your colleagues and your company depend on you, and you have a vested interest in doing the right thing for the company's profitability. Do the right thing, even when no one is watching.

KN: Very true, and I think our *Combat Finance* readers are hearing some recurring themes from our successful CFPD presenters. How has your military experience shaped your approach to your personal finances?
SS: *Budgeting. I learned to set priorities in the military. This includes living without things that I may want, but can't afford. I pay myself first—saving for retirement. Then, I pay my bills. Then, I buy the fun stuff. If I can't afford something extra, I don't buy it, I live without it, or I save for it; delayed gratification is all right.*

KN: Budgeting and being content to live within your means on the way to success. Outstanding. Tell us about the proudest moment of your military career and how you think it has affected you as an employee or business person.
SS: *Retirement. I retired from the military on May 15, 2007. I had transferred from active duty (Active Guard Reserve) to the traditional National Guard two years earlier to attend law school full-time. On May 15, 2007, I started my first legal job, as a summer associate for a law firm in Seattle, WA, where I worked between my second and third year of law school, and where I worked after graduation. That day, the senior partners took me to lunch. During our conversation at lunch, I mentioned that I was officially retiring from the military that day. They told me that other than my strong performance in law school, it was my 20 years of military service that led them to hire me—from a very deep and competitive pool of applicants. So, there I was, a civilian again; no uniform; no retirement ceremony; no fanfare. But, I had something far more valuable than the typical military pomp and circumstance. I had a "toolbox" full of unique and challenging management and leadership experiences that set the conditions for a successful life in the business world.*

KN: Would you tell us about the most difficult moment or experience in your military career and how you think it affected you as an employee or business person?
SS: *Ranger school graduation. Ranger school was the toughest, long-term, physical and mental challenge I faced as a young man—21 years*

old. There was no faking it . . . you could either hang with the program, or you could not. The standards and expectations were high. There was a very high drop-out/failure rate—over 70 percent. It was tough, and I felt like I really accomplished something when I graduated because I overcame a great deal of physical and mental adversity; one meal a day and about two hours of sleep a day for more than two months, while facing endless tactical challenges. I was very hungry and very tired. Since then, although things may seem tough at times, I know I have survived worse. Not only did I make it through, but I did well, and I felt good about experiencing and making it through the adversity; it was a rite of passage, in a sense. Now, I am able to keep stress and adversity at work and at home in proper perspective. I think to myself, hey this stinks, but I can eat what I want, and I'll probably get to sleep for more than two hours . . . so, it's not that bad. In the end, this experience taught me that I am tougher than I think I am, and that the satisfaction of surviving adversity is greater than the pain of the adversity itself.

KN: Nothing to it but to do it! What was the funniest or most embarrassing moment of your military career? What did you learn from that experience?

SS: *For one of the most embarrassing moments of my 20-year military career, I think back to being a Second Lieutenant in flight school. I was taking a check ride in an AH-1 Cobra Attack Helicopter. I, as luck would have it, drew the proverbial short straw and had to take my check ride with the company commander. The captain was having a bad day, and he seemingly took it out on me. From the start of the check ride I could do nothing right in his eyes. During the low-level tactical portion of the flight, I asked him to fly, and gave him the controls of the aircraft in order to plan the next phase of the flight. A few minutes later, while studying the map and calculating time/distance, I noticed that he was flying off the course I told him to fly. I corrected him and continued planning. A minute or so later I heard him screaming, and he began flying erratically, yelling that he "had been shot"—he apparently was faking an aerial ambush to make the check ride more interesting. I was not amused. Given that the instructors are supposed to cooperate as co-pilots, and the fact that I needed to complete my planning, I told him to grab the first aid kit and patch himself up, but to stay on* *course, because I needed to finish planning prior to crossing the next navigational check point. I finished planning, took the controls, and finished the remaining portion of the check ride in total silence; yes, he was now giving me the silent treatment. After landing, he jumped out of the aircraft and told me to meet him in his office. I completed the post flight and reported to his office to find the grumpy little captain sitting at his desk. I reported; he told me to sit down; I sat. He said, "I guess you know you failed that check ride—right?" I said what any good Second Lieutenant would say: "Yes Sir!" He gave me a weak lecture… but I was so surprised, I did not hear a word of it. I was quite embarrassed, to say the least; this was the first check ride I had failed in flight school, and the first "failure" I had experienced in my brief military career. Then, I reported to our class leader and told him that I had failed the check ride. He told me that I would be scheduled to take another check ride and to report back the next day. I knew that I was prepared, so I just went home and reviewed in preparation for the next day.*

The next morning, I reported for my follow-up, with my tail between my legs. I sat down wondering who would show up to give me the check ride. Along came a very senior Warrant Officer. He sat down and asked how I was doing. I said I was doing fine and asked him how he was doing. He said, "I'm having a really bad day, I didn't sleep well last night because my dog kept barking, and then as I was getting in the shower, I took my Rolex off and dropped it in the flushing toilet—gone forever." I thought to myself, "Great, here we go again." He told me he knew the captain had failed me the day before. Then he said, "Don't worry about it, that guy is a jerk; let's go fly and have some fun." We did. He put me through a thorough check ride, but it was challenging and fair, and I actually enjoyed it. That experience reinvigorated me throughout the remainder of flight school. After the check ride, he told me that I was a really good pilot. This was a great compliment—especially coming from a senior Warrant Officer.

First, I learned to really like Warrant Officers, and had great respect and professional relationships with many Warrant Officers during my entire career. But, I also learned not to be too hard on myself. I knew I was ready; I studied and worked hard prior to that check ride; I prepared and had done my best. But, I had the misfortune of a weak, insecure, grumpy check pilot. I got over it quickly and moved on—despite the embarrassment.

Those are some great lessons Steve, and I'm so glad that our *Combat Finance* readers got to hear from someone who has demonstrated tremendous success in both the military and business communities. It certainly demonstrates that great qualities and values are universal and lead to success in many types of endeavors. Thank you again for your service to our country and to the state of Nevada, and we wish you continued success in your current career.

Combat Finance readers, you can look forward to more CFPD as you move to the next chapters.

Great Leaders Delegate

I'm not going to tell you that presiding over your cabinet is going to be easy, but it's necessary because you can't be an expert at everything, nor do you have the time to do everything, just as no military commander could ever be an expert in every technical area within a large unit. We have to resist the urge to micromanage parts of our lives that may be best delegated to others who have the expertise in a certain area. For example, many investors start out obsessing over a single stock or mutual fund. They go over it again and again trying to determine if it's going to do well, when really, if they understood the big picture of asset allocation, they would know that this single investment is not how they're going to be successful. An amateur investor obsessing over one stock would be like a general focusing on which of two rifles to use. At the end of the day, as long as both rifles fire reliably in a similar fashion, that decision has very little impact on the course of a war or our ability to develop a top-notch military. It's very similar in investing. It's the discipline and process that are so important, not the specific investment. That's why, in *Combat Finance,* we've focused on behavioral changes, not individual investment recommendations. Our behavior and commitment to developing a process for success are the things we can and should control.

I am spending time emphasizing the importance of proper delegation because I see so many people rush in to do the work of their delegates the minute things go a little differently from what they would have done, and that's shortsighted. We must listen and absorb what our cabinet has to say. I've benefited from the knowledge of my own advisors so many times in my career. During a real-estate-investment deal recently, the lending bank said that I needed to increase my insurance coverage on the property. I called my agent to let him know the higher amount of coverage they were seeking, but instead of just quoting me the higher premium, he told me he wanted to take a more detailed look. He called me back and said that because I had coverage on both the main building and the outbuildings, I was completely covered for more than the amount they were requiring. He even called the bank directly and set them straight. I could've gone with insurance online to maybe get a better price, but there's no way they would've known enough about this project and volunteered the advice that saved me money.

Another time my cabinet saved me money was in a commercial property transaction that took place right around the same time. My CPA knew that I needed an appraisal on the property to establish a cost basis, since I had acquired the property through a foreclosure and not a sale. She took a look at the situation and was able to suggest that I have the bank I like to work with order the appraisal. That way, if I decided to pursue any financing to cover capital improvements, the bank would accept the appraisal rather than having to order another one. That piece of advice saved me nearly $3,500, which is more than my CPA's entire tax return bill for three years. I could not have looked that up online because I didn't know I needed to ask the question, but my CPA did. Her expertise was definitely more valuable than the price I paid for the advice.

Without choosing the correct experts in our lives and delegating to them effectively, we would never know what we don't know. We'll never understand what type of information we're operating without. I'm sure you can remember a time when you didn't know what you didn't know. Think about how that plays into your financial life. Find ways to bring experts into your fold, people you can trust with niche decisions that affect your portfolio, and people who can save you time so that you can focus on developing your financial nation. The right experts can change your outlook, apply new technology, and see patterns where you only see bursts of information. That kind of experience counts.

After Action Review

If you have finished this chapter successfully and have completed the following tasks, you are hereby promoted to Master Sergeant E-8 (MSG) in *Combat Finance*. You have:

1. Completed and maintained all key tasks from previous chapters.
2. Consistently followed your Combat Finance general orders.
3. Consistently maintained your financial bearing.
4. Completed your consumer debt pay-off plan from Chapter 1 and remained debt-free.
5. Calculated and built your reserves as described in Chapter 2.
6. Used the battlefield calculus described in Chapter 3 to budget for, save for, and purchase a home that you can defend in the face of financial attacks.
7. Established retirement savings of at least 10 percent of your income and made it automatic through payroll deduction or an automated weekly or monthly bank transfer.
8. Analyzed your insurance needs and purchased the prescribed minimums in Chapter 5.
9. Carefully developed your cabinet and communicated your strategic objectives to them:
   - **a.** Selected a secretary of defense, your primary financial advisor.
   - **b.** Selected your secretary of state, your attorney.
   - **c.** Selected your treasury secretary, your CPA.
   - **d.** Selected your director of homeland security, your insurance agent.
   - **e.** Clearly communicated strategic objectives to the selected cabinet secretaries.

If you have not completed each of the key tasks in this chapter, *continue reading,* but you are barred from promotion until you meet these minimum standards.

Chapter 7

Turning Your Strategic Objectives into Mission Statements

Although there is a lot of camaraderie in the military, because we truly respect each other, each of the branches likes to give the other a hard time. There are a few jokes that go around about pilots, and one of them in particular always gets the laughs: How do you know if the person you're talking to in a bar is a pilot? The answer: Don't worry, he'll tell you. And although we give pilots a hard time for their confidence, there is something that pilots are pretty darn great at doing, and that's planning. No pilot ever willingly starts a sortie without a detailed flight plan complete with primary targets, alternate targets, tertiary targets, desired effects, and an end state, as well as a slew of other preparedness steps. They create such detailed plans because they have to. What if we had fighter pilots flying around without specific engagement criteria, with no defined mission, and no fuel consumption plan? In best-case scenario terms, it would be a complete waste of resources. In worst-case scenario terms, that kind of disorganization could be extremely dangerous for the pilot, the civilian population on the ground, and to the mission itself.

The Fundamentals of Planning

Detailed planning creates a clear unity of effort that ensures that everyone is working toward the same goal. In this chapter, I'll be giving you an idea of what a mission statement looks like and how you can use it. I'll also use a few terms to help us navigate our mission statements, so bear with me while I give you some much-needed definitions, a mini-glossary of sorts:

- *Strategic objective:* A primary goal, such as retirement or college expenses, whose success is necessary for the individual's or family's overall vision to be realized. *Goal* or just *objective* for short.
- *Mission:* A clearly articulated assignment, generally intended to achieve or help achieve a larger goal or objective.
- *Mission statement:* Clarifies the objective or goal and describes *how* it will be accomplished by articulating "who, what, where, when, and why."
- *Purpose:* The broader reason for which a task is being undertaken. Explains *why* we're participating in this mission.
- *Key tasks:* The mission-critical steps necessary to reach your desired end state. If key tasks are not completed, the mission will fail.
- *End state:* The fairy tale ending. What *right* should look like when everything in the plan comes to fruition.

You'll need all these terms to understand the kind of planning you're going to undertake in this chapter. First, we'll list our strategic objectives, then we'll craft mission statements for those goals, and finally, we'll communicate those goals to our cabinet. This kind of planning is key to your financial success, and without it you will never clearly articulate your desired end state, let alone accomplish it. After all, if you aren't clear about where you are going, how do you get there?

We embrace a similar emphasis on planning in the army. No army commander would ever willingly commence an operation without giving the units below him a mission statement. A commander takes his strategic objective and communicates it in a mission statement outlining who, what, when, where, and why, using exact, precise terminology. The goal might be to defeat, or to destroy, or to occupy—each one carrying a unique distinction. By clearly articulating the goal, the commander makes it clear what he wants from his subordinate units. The mission will usually be accompanied by a purpose, key tasks, and an end state, which could be anything from denying the use of a terrain to making civilians safe to making sure everyone makes it from one point to another. That kind of clarity ensures that all units are working toward a common goal with a maximum unity of effort. Through that planning, we know that everyone understands what we're trying to accomplish on any given day. We want to preserve our resources so that instead of fanning our efforts out over a huge area, we can concentrate on what's most important, which helps us get there faster and more efficiently. This kind of planning makes it possible for us, when things go wrong, to easily transition to a contingency plan, because we know that even if our key tasks vary, we'll still have our purpose and end state in mind.

Some of you may be wondering why planning is so important. Although there are many reasons, one of the biggest is human nature. Specifically I'm talking about the part of human nature that will always weigh the *present* more heavily than the future. In other words, we often confuse *urgent* with *important*. As a *Combat Finance* reader, I want you to have a crystal clear understanding of the difference between the two. For example, if you like to clothes shop, you must understand that the new shirt you spotted might seem urgent, but it is not important unless you don't already have a shirt. The new shirt is certainly not more important than your child's college education. But human nature is such that because the shirt is right there in front of us and the college education is years away, most people will buy the shirt and forgo the college fund contribution that month. That's soup sandwich, and I want you to be better than that. I'm going to walk you through a process you can use to ensure that you plan for and fund the important things first. But get it out of your head that financial planning is all about sacrifices. If you do it right, it's about taking care of the most important things before the urgent things, and then enjoying your life with the rest of your income. Like Austin Powers said, "Freedom *and* responsibility. It's a very groovy time."

How do we ensure that we are taking care of the most important goals first and still know if we can simultaneously buy those new shoes at the mall or new tools at the home improvement store? To explain this, we need to review where we have been. In basic training, we paid off our debts. Reserves taught us to be ready for emergencies and changing situations. FOB Mayor taught us not to overspend on our home. Training taught us that this is a lifelong process, not a short-term financial fix. Protecting the home front made sure that we are covered for catastrophic situations. The value of advice taught us that we need a strong team. And now, strategic objectives will help us take the vague notions of what we want financially and help us turn those into quantifiable, actionable mission statements. Once we have begun to fully implement each of our missions we will know if we have enough left over for the more trivial, but seemingly urgent, wants in our lives. My guess is that you will still be able to afford many of the wants in your life, and that you will actually enjoy them more knowing that they are not being purchased at the expense of your more important goals.

KEY TASK 1: Make a list of all of your primary strategic objectives and prioritize them in order of importance. Note: If retirement is not first on the list, I'm going to order you to change it.

Consider all your financial priorities and make a list of them. Everyone has different financial goals and objectives, but some examples include college savings, a vacation home, a recreational vehicle, a boat, travel, or assisting your grandkids with their education. Remember, you paid your debts in Chapter 1 and built your reserves in Chapter 2, so you can leave those off this list, but you must remain debt free and maintain your reserves going forward. The one thing that absolutely must be at the top of this list is retirement. If you're prioritizing your children's college education over your own financial well-being later in life, you need to take a hard look at how comfortable your kids would be if you were living with them during your later years. That is soup sandwich.

Make retirement the top of your list and then work down. If you teach your kids good morals, values, and work ethic, they are going to be just fine, so focus on that and your retirement first.

Sometimes it can be helpful to rank each of these priorities individually on the list from 1 to 10 to indicate how important they are to you. We do this in my financial practice. After completing the ranking, we discuss it and, usually, if anyone rates something at a five or below, it turns out to be a want, not a need. That doesn't mean that you can't achieve it; we just don't focus on wants until needs are adequately funded. This kind of prioritizing will allow you to really re-emphasize where your efforts should be concentrated. You have to make time in your busy schedules as a family to determine what your goals are and agree as a family on the rankings of those goals. This can be hard because the new garage might be important to him, but the vacation is important to her. You have to discuss choices and consequences. Regular, respectful, and fulfilling communication is key to accomplish this first key task. I know this is difficult to do sometimes, but having those discussions will bring your family closer together. Guys, do you understand how much your spouse will appreciate that you budgeted both time and money for a family vacation? Gals, do you know how great it is for a guy to have his "man cave" in the garage guilt free because you both know there is a plan in action to cover the high-priority items first?

Examples of primary strategic objectives:

- Retire at age 65 with $5,000 per month income in 2013 dollars.
- Accumulate enough to cover 75 percent of in-state public university expenses in 13 years.
- Save $40,000 within the next five years to buy a new car.
- Save $5,000 per year for a family travel fund.

List your primary strategic objectives in order of priority:

1. ______________________________
2. ______________________________
3. ______________________________
4. ______________________________
5. ______________________________

KEY TASK 2: Create a mission statement for each of your strategic objectives.

We must prioritize our financial goals, and then we must turn those goals into mission statements that are clear, concise, quantifiable, and achievable. Look at each of the priorities you listed earlier and plan your approach to each of those goals. Each one needs to have a mission statement, including key tasks and end state.

Here is one example of what a mission statement could look like:

Title: Retirement
Who: Bob (40) and Sally (38) Jones
What: Establish retirement resources sufficient to generate $5,000 per month in lifetime income in 2013 dollars.
Where: Social Security and qualified retirement plans: 401(k), IRA, Roth, and others.
When: No later than Bob's 67th birthday.
Why/Purpose: To ensure a level of retirement income that will allow us to spend time with grandchildren, travel to see family and friends, and to give back to our community through volunteer work.
Key task 1: Work with primary financial advisor to estimate social security income, military pension, and employer pensions to determine the likely amounts that those will contribute.
Key task 2: Work with primary financial advisor to estimate monthly investment contributions needed to meet the difference between the income in Key Task 1 and $5,000 (in 2013 dollars).
Key task 3: Initiate automatic deductions to 401(k), IRAs, Roths, and other investments as recommended by our primary financial advisor in task 2 to meet that mission.
Key task 4: Meet with primary financial advisor at least once per year to reevaluate required savings, asset allocation, and any changes to the mission, and so on.
End state: We (Bob and Sally) retire with qualified retirement assets necessary to provide a comfortable and prudent lifetime income that utilizes conservative withdrawal rates so we can comfortably absorb the economic ups and downs that will certainly occur during our retirement. Initiating the key tasks and conducting regular reviews will allow us to enjoy our lives knowing that we are on track.

Here is a second example of what a mission statement could look like:

Title: College expense
Who: The Jones family, specifically Mariah (age 5).
What: Create a college savings account sufficient to cover 75 percent of expected in-state total expenses (tuition, fees, books, room and board) for four years.
Where: Qualified educational savings programs and accounts such as 529 plans, Education IRAs, and others.
When: No later than the 2026 fall semester.
Why/Purpose: To ensure that if Mariah prepares herself academically to attend college, she will be able to do so debt free through these savings, scholarships, grants, and part-time work.
Key task 1: Work with primary financial advisor to estimate the monthly investment amounts needed to meet the mission.
Key task 2: Initiate automatic monthly investments to Education IRA, 529 Plans, prepaid tuition programs, and others as recommended by primary financial advisor.
Key task 3: Meet with primary financial advisor at least annually to reevaluate required savings, asset allocation, changes to mission, and so forth.
Key task 4: Beginning around age 12 to 13, bring Mariah to the meetings to discuss her college accounts to teach her about finances, the trade-offs between different schools, their costs, and so forth.
End state: Mariah is not only financially and academically prepared for college, but is years ahead of her peers in understanding money, budgets, and cost-benefit analysis.

These mission statements will assist you in planning for your priority goals. If we all know that we have to plan to reach our goals, why don't we always do it? Well, I think it's pretty overwhelming for a lot of us. There's a reason a vacation is easier to plan for than retirement. Retirement is a decades-long plan that hinges on many contingencies. Our well-being is on the line. A vacation is a few days per year, involving a relatively small amount of money, and its end state is usually pretty clear: to have fun. Planning for a large financial goal can seem very overwhelming in comparison. And because of that, many families put it off, and just throw money into a 401(k) hoping that it will eventually work out without any meaningful direction. But hoping that it happens is neither a plan nor a strategy.

Writing a mission statement and communicating it to your cabinet will provide clarity, and only clarity will allow for unity of effort. It doesn't have to be a dissertation; it just has to quantify and clearly articulate what you are trying to accomplish. The end state guides us and allows us to adjust. If you know where you're going, it's easier to tell if the road in front of you is taking you there.

When it comes to planning for retirement or any large financial goal, it's important to annually revisit our goals. While I was in Afghanistan, both the squadron staff and the brigade staff above us revisited plans and looked at actual data versus what we had assumed in our planning models. We made adjustments as needed, based on evidence of effectiveness. We didn't just make a plan, memorize it, and throw the paper copy in the trash. Your cabinet of experts is going to help you review and revise your plans in a similar way. As long as you simply set up a meeting with them each year to review your strategic objectives and any life changes—pregnancy, marriage, divorce, school, and so forth—you're well on the way to maintaining effective progress. Technology and additional data make it easier every year for those of us in the financial planning industry to address contingencies, so take advantage of that by reviewing your plans with your financial professionals on an annual basis.

When something shiny comes along and tempts us to veer away from a financial priority, having a plan in place will prompt us to pause and assess whether it gets us to the desired end state. Getting distracted does not make you an idiot. It makes you human. We all have things in our lives that take our attention away from what we should be focused on accomplishing. Smart humans just put processes into place that help them accomplish those tasks more efficiently. Planning assists us in these tasks. This is important to me because I see clients get so sidetracked by these shiny things in situations where they don't have the resources to do so. Maybe a friend has a slam-dunk real estate opportunity or a family member wants them to invest in a business deal. They can very easily lose sight of the big picture and commit funds that really should have gone toward retirement, college, and other worthy goals. The more planning you do, the easier it will be to decide what you want to do when you are faced with something that could be a distraction. It will give you the decision-making power to differentiate between a great opportunity and a sidetracking journey. And sometimes you should take advantage of speculative investment opportunities, but only if you are tracking properly toward your primary goals, and only if the funds you are considering are over and above those needed to meet your goals. As long as these opportunities don't derail your main mission (retirement or college savings), then you may want to take some speculative risks now and then, but you need to conduct thorough planning first, so that you know if you can afford to take the risk.

Remember, as *Combat Finance* readers, I want you to take calculated risks and cut a buck loose once in a while, but only with those funds that are over and above that which is necessary to reach your primary strategic objectives. The only way you will reasonably know if the money you are considering using is truly excess is to work closely with your cabinet to figure that out. But here is the great part, once you take the time to plan and know that you are on track, now you can spend, have fun, and be more carefree with the rest of your income because you have taken the worry and fear out of whether or not you are taking care of the important things first.

KEY TASK 3: Meet with your cabinet secretaries to communicate your strategic objectives and mission statements to ensure unity of effort. Establish an annual review process thereafter.

Planning isn't just about the creation of a plan, but also the maintenance and execution of that plan. That process should include a detailed mission statement (as we discussed earlier) for each strategic objective, which your cabinet will help you develop and implement. It should also include a review process with family and your selected cabinet of experts to determine if you need any adjustments. Each year, you should meet first with your family to reevaluate your strategic objectives, and then meet with your cabinet. This is important because you don't want to abdicate your responsibility to oversee the folks that work for you. You should ask: Are we on track? Is everything we talked about last year on track? Are we achieving our goals? How is our portfolio performance? How is our asset allocation? What are your fees this year? The advisor is going to want to know whether there were any changes to your strategic objectives this year, whether there were any big life changes, whether there need to be changes to your key tasks, and whether there were any changes to your timelines to get things done. You should discuss performance, changes to objectives or targets, efficiencies (especially regarding taxes), beneficiaries, and any new business to name a few. These meetings shouldn't be overwhelming, but simply a way to assess your progress and make adjustments as necessary.

Sample Advisor Review Questions/Discussion Points

Has there been a change in the family?

- Divorce
- Death
- Marriage
- Birth

Has there been a change in your finances?

- Sold/bought a home
- Received an inheritance
- Major medical expenses
- Changed jobs/position
- Adult children living back at home
- Parent(s) in assisted living or living at home
- Selling/sold your business

Has there been a change in retirement plans?

- Retiring earlier/later
- Willing to work part-time
- Relocating

Major concerns

- Tax-related concerns
- Will/trust updates
- Investment volatility/allocation

There's a saying that no military plan survives the first contact. You can make a great plan, but once the bullets start flying, it never goes exactly as you imagined, even with significant research and time invested. And yet, we still need to plan for each strategic objective and the contingencies that may arise. We assess our courses of action based on how we think the enemy will act or react. In the military we plan so that we can react to contact and still work toward an understood end state. In the same way, as investors, we have to have a base plan that has room to react to the market, the economy, changes in our careers and families, and so forth. Things don't always go as planned in investing, but that's never an excuse not to have a plan to begin with. It's so much easier to adjust from a base plan than to be working with no deliberate mission from the start. In the process of planning, you will change and evolve your operating procedures because you'll identify flaws and obstacles that may arise. The process of planning is nearly as valuable as the plan itself, because that's where you have those "'ah-ha" moments of clarity that will help you deal with issues when they arise.

Many of my clients come in and initially resist planning because they believe that since things always change, there is no way to accurately plan. Why should we spend a bunch of time planning for something that's not going to happen exactly as we think? Well, it's true that no plan will ever fully survive first contact or your first big life change or emergency. But, you're still better off with a base plan from which you can adjust. Let's say, for example, that you have to move fuel and supplies from Kabul, Afghanistan, to Mehtar Lam, which is where I was based. If you plan for it, you'll know the driving distance, the manpower you'll probably need, and the basic terrain you'll face. But you will definitely face contingencies. That could be anything from an IED, an ambush, road closures, or inclement weather. You can't make an exact plan for those, but in the process of developing a primary plan, you can start to identify the risk and process of dealing with these types of conditions, which may or may not pop up. By doing basic planning, you will have sat down with your second in command to discuss the difficulties that you may face. Then he or she will sit down with the intelligence officer, who will present the likely enemy courses of action. Then the operations officer will talk through how you would react to that because he's in charge of tactical operations.

Some Days Are Better Than Others

Sometimes trying to save one investment will cost you another. Cut your losses and walk away when you have to, but never give up the overall fight and always stick to the fundamentals.

This type of war-gaming—identifying, brainstorming, and role-playing possible outcomes—ensures that not only do you have a primary plan, but you will be able to modify it on the fly if you need to. In addition, the process itself makes you think through the bad things that might happen so you are more likely to act decisively and confidently than to react in fear when things do happen. Each person in the unit is now clear on the end state and can act appropriately to prepare her area for problems. Even if something comes at you that you didn't discuss, it's not going to be completely out of the blue because of all the scenarios you walked through. So saying that we shouldn't plan because no plan survives first contact is not an excuse. Just because you don't know what interest rates are going to be when you retire or we don't know what Social Security payments will be doesn't relieve us of the obligation to plan. Regardless of how things change, we can act more efficiently in the future when these things do become more clear if we have a base plan. You and your cabinet will have talked about your plan in the case of high inflation, economic recession, or other obstacles. What we do face may not be exactly what we planned for, but we'll be able to react better than someone who didn't plan at all.

Combat Finance Professional Development (CFPD)

Combat Finance readers, welcome back to combat finance professional development training. Once again we are going to broaden our experience, this time by bringing in a retired Air Force Brigadier General who also served 13 years of enlisted service. I first met Brigadier General Bob Fitch in Mehtar Lam, Afghanistan, when he came to visit us during our deployment. At that time he was the commander of the Nevada Air National Guard, and they had a unit deployed to Bagram Airfield, so after he visited his unit he flew over to Laghman to visit us. Since we're a cavalry unit, we don't like giving PowerPoint slideshows when the real thing is right out the front door, so we asked Brigadier General Fitch if we could take him on a patrol to the bazaar in Laghman. Since the commander and I and a handful of senior officers and NCOs were the only ones who knew he was coming, we figured it was safe. When he said yes and we went to get the patrol ready, we were giving high fives—in Nevada even our Air Guard Brigadier Generals would rather get out with the locals than sit in an office. We had a great patrol, and Brigadier General Fitch has told me several times since, that it was the highlight of his trip. We are fortunate to have such a fine officer, who also had a very successful civilian career working for Nevada's main power utility, join our discussion. So take a look at what he has to share, and apply it to your career and your finances.

Name: Brigadier General (BG) (R) Robert V. Fitch, Air Force
Total years of service: 42.5

KN: How old were you when you first began your military service?
RF: *19.*

KN: Which branch did you enlist/commission into, and why did you choose that branch of service?
RF: *I chose the Nevada Air National Guard because of my love for flying and working around airplanes. I was enlisted for 13 years, then received my commission.*

KN: Those years of enlisted service certainly add depth to your background and experiences. Thinking back to basic training, describe some of your experiences.
RF: *Thinking back 43 years is a stretch, but I believe the fear factor that they could really hurt you physically and mentally was all I needed.*

KN: Yes, I suppose the latitude the drill instructors took back then was much different than today. Which values have you learned in the military that have made you a better employee or business person?
RF: *Duty, Honor, Country. Always deliver on your commitments and lead by example.*

Here is an excerpt from a speech I gave at my first Commander's Call. These three words have always inspired me and are ones I attempt to live by:

1. Nobility. *Remember, each of us volunteered to be in this unit. Not one of us was drafted or was required to be here. Whether you came here to get help with school, for the career opportunity, or the reputation of the unit, we're all in the same boat. Being in the military is a calling. Each of us has been called to continue the tradition of one of the foundations of this country, serving in the U.S. military. This is one of the few institutions that have been in place since the founding of this nation. That's why our core values, Integrity First, Service Before Self, and Excellence in All We Do, matter so much. It's an honor and a privilege to serve the past, present, and future citizens of this nation. Every time you put on*

your uniform, deploy, or just drive through those front gates, think about the nobility of what you've been trained to do. We serve and protect the United States of America, the citizens of Nevada, and all the members of our external and internal families. Service and Nobility go hand in hand.

2. Legacy. *Each of us stands upon the shoulders of some man or woman who helped build this great organization we call the Nevada Air National Guard. Our unit has an outstanding reputation because of the hard work of those who came before us. Each of us has a responsibility and an obligation to leave this place better than we found it. A legacy is what stays in place after we leave. It's about adding value, making a difference, and leaving a mark. Every day you come onto this base, you make the choice of what legacy you're going to leave. This is based upon your attitude, your character, and your competence. Make the choice to raise the bar, to be a best practice, to role model the attributes of an outstanding airman, to demonstrate the pride of serving in this great organization, and I can guarantee, your legacy will be etched in stone, and future generations will appreciate the successes that you've left in place.*
3. Leadership. *Each and every person on this base is a leader. Leadership is the ability to exercise influence. Leadership is the capacity to influence others through inspiration motivated by a passion, generated by a vision, produced by a conviction, ignited by a purpose. I want each of you to influence those around you in a positive way. I want to you be an inspiration in everything you do. I want each person to be motivated by a passion to do your jobs to the best of your ability. I want you to look into the future and see the outstanding opportunities that your career has to offer. And I want you to live your life with purpose and meaning.*

If you can remember these three words, in all of your thoughts, actions, and deeds as an airman, Nobility, Legacy, and Leadership, and practice those on a regular basis, then we'll all walk away from this organization with our heads held high, knowing that we've done our calling well.

KN: Nobility, Legacy and Leadership; those are great things to strive toward. I also like that you began with Duty, Honor, Country. That was my platoon's motto in basic training, which we had to yell out every time we were called to attention. I think I have yelled those words at least a thousand times, yet they are still so powerful if we live by them. How has your military experience shaped your approach to your personal finances?
RF: *Always deliver on your commitments. Don't spend what you don't have.*

KN: You sound like a *Combat Finance* reader, sir! Tell me about the proudest moment of your military career.
RF: *Being selected as the Commander of the Nevada Air National Guard.*

KN: Congratulations on your command, sir. That is a real honor. Tell me about the most difficult moment or experience in your military career and how you think it affected you as an employee or business person.
RF: *I relieved three colonels of their command in one day. Always do the right thing even if it comes at a personal cost to you. Never doubt your personal convictions.*

KN: It's true; the easy decisions are never the ones that define you. What was the funniest or most embarrassing moment of your military career? What did you learn from that experience?
RF: *My most embarrassing moment came when I was unprepared to conduct a briefing in Germany! I thought I could talk my way through it, but it didn't work out well....*

Brigadier General Fitch, thank you so much for sharing your experiences with us. Delivering on your commitments, not spending what you don't have, and believing in your convictions among others. These are all great lessons that we can take back and apply toward our own lives, careers, and financial goals. Congratulations again on your outstanding career of service to the United States Air Force, the Nevada Air National Guard, and to our nation.

"A" Way

There are many people who plan their missions and conduct simultaneous operations effectively leading up to their retirement. One of my favorite planning success stories is a client who is an airline pilot who planned so thoroughly that even when a challenge came out of the blue, she'd set herself up to be able to change course and react. She was a former air force pilot and spent time flying in the reserves after active duty. Shortly after I started working with her, she was promoted to fly the San Francisco to Tokyo leg for a major airline. It was a huge pay raise and a prestigious promotion. Then September 11th hit. Everyone in the airline and travel industries cut back, and her employer went through a bankruptcy. Her pension was gutted, and she was demoted to a regional route for the airline because she was young and had so little seniority. Her pay was cut by nearly 60 percent.

But she had planned for obstacles and contingencies. Her plan? Like me, she saved every one of her reserve checks and set them aside in savings. She lived on half her income all the time and maxed out her airline 401(k) contributions, even though she was eligible for a pension because she knew that airlines were historically volatile and she wanted to be sure that she had her retirement covered even if her pension didn't pan out. She also contributed to a ROTH during the years that her income was not above the maximum eligible amount. She lived so well within her means going into her company's difficulties that she handled the cut well. She knew when she started to fly that she would have to retire at the age of 55, which was mandated at the time by the Federal Aviation Administration, so she planned for retirement aggressively from the outset knowing that she wouldn't have as much time as other people to save. (The FAA retirement age has since been changed to 65.) She set herself up with careful financial planning to be in a good place before she hit retirement age. She worked her way back up and now flies that very same overseas route that was taken away from her after September 11th. She's doing better than ever, and that's because she had built her reserves, knew not to spend her full paycheck, reviewed her plans each year with professionals, and systematically invested in her retirement. That kind of success only comes with careful, repetitive *Combat Finance* planning. And you can do that, too.

After Action Review

If you have finished this chapter successfully and have completed the following tasks, you are hereby promoted to Sergeant Major E-9 (SGM) in *Combat Finance*. You have:

1. Completed and maintained all key tasks from previous chapters.
2. Consistently followed your *Combat Finance* general orders.
3. Consistently maintained your financial bearing.
4. Completed your consumer debt pay-off plan from Chapter 1 and remained debt free.
5. Calculated and built your reserves as described in Chapter 2.
6. Used the battlefield calculus described in Chapter 3 to budget for, save for, and purchase a home that you can defend in the face of financial attacks.
7. Established retirement savings of *at least* 10 percent of your income and made it automatic through payroll deduction or an automated weekly or monthly bank transfer.
8. Analyzed your insurance needs and purchased the prescribed minimums in Chapter 5.
9. Carefully developed your cabinet using Chapter 6 as a guide.
10. Turned each strategic objective into an actionable mission statement:
    a. Listed all primary strategic objectives and prioritize them in order of importance.
    b. Created a mission statement for each of your strategic objectives.
    c. Met with your cabinet secretaries to communicate your strategic objectives and mission statements to ensure unity of effort.

If you have not completed each of the key tasks in this chapter, *continue reading,* but you are barred from promotion until you meet these minimum standards.

Chapter 8

Build Your Armed Forces, Not a Gun Collection

As a financial advisor, I spend many hours talking to people about investing. But whether I'm at a cocktail party, at a Rotary Club meeting, or getting my haircut, I also spend a lot of time listening. I hear a lot of talk about short-term issues like interest rates and the upcoming Fed meeting, or what is happening with the price of gold this week, but very rarely do I hear people talk about what their strategic approach is to asset allocation. Inevitably, most people want to talk about what they should buy and what's hot right now. I listen politely, of course, but my perspective on this is always the same: Stop trying to build a gun collection. Instead, focus on what your strategic objectives are and then select the investment allocation that will give you the highest probability of achieving those goals.

What do I mean by that? Let me try to explain it this way. Maybe you have a friend, as I do, who has a really great gun collection. Of all the guns my friend has, my favorite one to shoot is his silenced automatic .22, because you just pull the trigger and you barely hear the rounds going out; you just watch the target shred. It's so much fun to shoot that I could see why a person could get really caught up in buying great guns like that. If you are a gun enthusiast, and you have the funds available, after covering all the important things we discussed in previous chapters, then there is nothing wrong with building a gun collection. But the gun collectors I know are very rational people, and they know that it is just a gun collection. They don't fool themselves into thinking they have a well-equipped and trained militia ready to hire themselves out on missions like some foreign legion. It's just a gun collection, and they know it.

In stark contrast to building a gun collection, the U.S. Department of Defense takes an entirely different approach to strategic planning. First the President establishes his priorities and communicates them to his cabinet, specifically the Secretary of Defense. Then the Secretary of Defense turns around and publishes guidance for each of the branch chiefs to follow. They then turn around and issue guidance down the chain of command to ensure that each branch of service is working toward fulfilling the President's strategic objectives. They will do this by setting short, intermediate, and long-term goals and benchmarks to ensure that they are making progress as planned. One of the more recent policy guidance documents was released in January of 2012 entitled *Sustaining U.S. Global Leadership: Priorities for 21st Century Defense.* In this document, the President provides a letter outlining his strategic objectives. Next, the Secretary of Defense provides a statement describing what the Joint Force will work toward in order to meet the President's objectives. Finally, the document contains an update of the current situation, key missions that must be accomplished, and guidance about how to achieve the desired end state. From this guidance, a unity of effort can now take place as each branch works to achieve the goals set forth. Does any of this sound familiar? That's right Daniel-son, Mr. Miyagi has been teaching you a little wax-on, wax-off in previous chapters.

The parallel to investing is that many people spend their energies trying to build a hot stock collection in their financial lives. They don't focus on what the strategic objective is and what missions need to be accomplished to get there. They then often fail to communicate their objectives to their secretary of defense so that she can help them build a diversified, effective force to accomplish them. Instead they get distracted by every hot new "gun" out there and go chasing after it. But how is that hot new weapon going to help you build your armed forces to accomplish your military's mission and reach your strategic objectives? The truth is you have no idea if you haven't considered that mission prior to your gun search and certainly well before your gun purchase. Chasing the hot stock first is backwards behavior, and that's soup sandwich.

Investors must change their focus from "What's hot?" to "What is my mission for this portion of my money?" When you understand that mission, you can select a combination of forces, weapons, and equipment that most effectively meets those requirements. Good financial advisors have seen the folly of having 20 battleships in one portfolio, or worse yet, buying one great big battleship. They have seen the problem with picking up a .50 caliber weapon here and a silenced .22 there. They know that trying to put those weapons together into a top-notch force will be highly ineffective, unless they take their clients' mission into account first.

Asset Allocation Fundamentals

Asset allocation is the mix of stocks, bonds, real estate, and other alternative investments that allow us to spread out our money and cushion us from severe downturns in the value of any one asset class. It is also the process of rebalancing your investments between those different asset classes when opportunities present themselves in the marketplace. For example, when stocks fell sharply in 2008 and early 2009, other assets went up, allowing investors who were diversified to take some of their profits on things like treasury bonds and put money into stocks that were down. When stocks began recovering in price in March 2009, and continuing almost uninterrupted through the writing of this book in 2013, investors who had taken advantage of their diversification by rebalancing did very well. What was a very tough time for many became an opportunity for those who followed *Combat Finance* principles. If investors had kept their financial bearing by maintaining adequate reserves, had kept themselves debt free, and were in a defendable home that allowed them to have money left over to invest every month, they probably did just fine in the downturn. If they also had a well-diversified portfolio that allowed them to buy assets at bargain prices using profits from holdings that were up and allowed their dividends and interest to reinvest throughout the downturn, they came out the other side of the great recession in better shape than when it started. They accumulated more shares at cheaper prices than they ever would have been able to had the market not come down. I'm not advocating for tough markets because many people who don't follow the *Combat Finance* principles were hurt financially, but what I am saying is that if you keep your financial bearing at all times and are well diversified, you will learn not to fear tough markets but to see opportunity in them instead.

One of the great Wall Street thinkers and a man whom I greatly admire when it comes to teaching the art and science of asset allocation is David Darst. In his book, *The Little Book That Saves Your Assets: What the Rich Do to Stay Wealthy in Up and Down Markets,* David says this:

> For centuries, fortunes have been made, preserved, or lost because people either paid careful attention to, or ignored, the main tenets of asset allocation. From Joseph in the Old Testament, through the Greeks, the Romans, the Venetians, the Spanish, and others, to the great banking fortunes of the Barings and the Rothschilds, and up to the Modern Era—Astor, Rockefeller, Carnegie, DuPont, and now Gates and Buffett, money has been *created* through concentration, and then compounded, accumulated, and *retained* by following the key ideas of asset allocation: diversification, rebalancing, risk management, and reinvestment. By the same token, mighty empires have fallen and fortunes have withered away when families and nations have let themselves get too concentrated in one kind of asset and thus far too exposed to risk.

David's book is outstanding, and since *Combat Finance* readers need to be committed to lifelong learning, I want you to put it on your reading list and finish it soon after you finish this book. You'll be a better and wiser steward of your family's finances if you do. But for now, since you have an idea of what asset allocation is, let's use another military analogy to better understand the concept and how it works to help you do all of the wonderful things David mentioned.

In many ways, asset allocation to include diversification, rebalancing, risk management, and reinvestment is exactly what the secretary of defense does all the time. As a country we maintain highly diversified armed forces made up of the army, navy, air force, and marines. Then within each of those branches we have an even greater diversification of capabilities and unique strengths. We do this because there is no single magic weapon or superhero that can handle every possible threat we may face. The most motivated soldier in the world is not going to keep our shipping lanes free from piracy. The most talented air force pilot in the world is not going to be able to teach investigation techniques to the Afghan National Police from her jet at 10,000 feet. Therefore, we must have this incredible depth of capabilities within our armed forces in order to accomplish our nation's strategic objectives, and we must rebalance them from time to time to keep pace with the current enemy situation. We must also conduct constant risk management while reinvesting in our personnel and equipment in order to keep them on the cutting edge of war-fighting skills and technology advances. When we think about diversification in the military this way, it's completely logical, and it makes sense to most people. So let's think about our investment asset allocation the same way. You are back to being the president of your financial nation, and you have set out your strategic objectives to your cabinet. Once you have done that, you are now sitting with your secretary of defense and looking at the capabilities of the army, navy, air force, and marines. You know that they each bring different capabilities to the fight, but what are they? To help you fully understand this discussion, you can reference Table 8.1 as you read about each branch of service.

Army

For this analogy I've chosen to draw a parallel between bonds, which are also referred to as fixed-income assets, and the army, because the army is great at securing terrain with infantry, armor, artillery, and all those ground-focused forces. The army is good at going into an area

Table 8.1 Asset Allocation Analogy

Army	*Bonds and Fixed Income* The Army is good at going in, overtaking forces, and occupying ground, but it takes a while for the Army to mobilize and get forces from place to place. A light infantry unit on foot only moves a few miles a day. Bonds are similar: The income on bonds is very slow and steady, but very reliable. The Army has different capabilities within its divisions: infantry, armor, field artillery, military police, or medical corps. This is the same with bonds; there are government bonds, corporate bonds, floating rate bonds, international bonds, long-term bonds, immediate-term bonds, short-term bonds, and so on. Even within your bonds, you have to pay attention to diversification. When you buy a bond, you are basically loaning money to whoever the bond issuer is. The bond pays a set amount of interest, and the principal is paid back, too, at the end of the bond term.
Navy	*Domestic Stocks–U.S. Stocks* The Navy has powerful forces that can move very quickly. Fast-moving carrier groups and battleships can use their far-ranging strike capabilities in a short amount of time. The Navy is much more capable of projecting force and thus is offensive in nature. It does give up a little more ground than the army, so when the economy goes into recessions, U.S. stocks don't hold the kind of ground that bonds potentially can. The Navy has submarines, carrier groups, frigates, battleships, and all sorts of diversified forces. Stocks are similar. There are small cap, intermediate cap, large cap, technology, utility, and so on, which have varied capabilities. Money should be diversified into the various sectors. It would be hard to imagine the Secretary of the Navy claiming the Navy would only focus on aircraft carriers.
Air Force	*International Stocks* The Air Force can get places very quickly. They have long-range bomber, surveillance, and other capabilities. They can be defensive through their ability to fend off other air forces, but they aren't particularly useful in holding a large amount of ground or keeping insurgents out of houses. They have great offensive capabilities, too, and that is why we want them in our portfolios. The Air Force enhances the strength of the Army and Navy, but they have certain unique capabilities that are very much needed in a well-rounded armed force.

	With international stocks, there will be different countries that have different volatilities and growth patterns within the companies that do business there. We need all these forms of diversification.
Marines	*Alternative Investments* Hedge funds, commodities, and real estate (among others) are alternative investments. These are much more volatile than other asset categories and are often risky because markets in these categories tend to rise quickly and fall quickly. The Marines are great at going into a risky situation hard and fast and can make a big difference in very dangerous combat missions. You never want the marines to be your sole portfolio because of the risk, even though they can be extremely productive.

of operation, overtaking enemy forces, and occupying that ground. But it does take the army a while to mobilize and to get forces built up to move from place to place. After all, tanks and Humvees and Bradleys are difficult to transport around the globe, so it takes a while to get large scale army forces into the fight. A light infantry unit can be mobilized and flown into the area of operations faster, but once they jump out of the plane, they are on foot. An infantry unit on foot is very effective at holding the ground they are on, but they can only travel a few miles a day. Bonds are similar in that they generally hold their ground when it comes to capital preservation, but they are not your fastest-moving asset when it comes to growing your portfolio. When you buy a bond, you're basically loaning money to whoever the bond issuer is. If it's a government bond, then you're loaning money to the government that issued the bond. There are also corporate bonds issued by all kinds of businesses like auto companies and utilities. When you loan these governments or corporations money in the form of a bond, they must pay a set amount of interest on that loan and pay back the principal at the end of the bond term. So the income on this type of investment, which we call fixed income because of the fixed rate of interest, is very slow and steady, but also very reliable for investors as long as the issuer of the bond is a financially solid entity. Just as the army has different capabilities within its different divisions—infantry, armor, field artillery, military police, medical corps and so on—so, too, do bonds. Government bonds, corporate bonds, floating-rate bonds, international bonds, long-term bonds, immediate-term bonds, short-term bonds, and others also have distinct capabilities and characteristics. Even within the army, or your bonds, you'll have to pay attention to your diversification and ensure that you have the right mix of capabilities for the mission at hand, just as the secretary of defense would have to be crazy to abandon the Navy, the Air Force, and the Marines and put the nation's entire defense budget in the Army. So, too, would the Secretary of the Army be crazy to put the entire budget of the army into tanks or artillery when a diversified force consisting of infantry, tanks, artillery, cavalry, signal, and transportation can be combined to be far stronger than any one of those entities working by themselves. Do the same thing with your bond portfolio by working with your advisor to select the right mix of bonds for your mission.

Navy

For the Navy I've chosen to draw a parallel with domestic stocks. A domestic stock is just a fancy way of saying an American-based company. Why do I think the Navy is a good way to explain this asset class? Because the navy has some really powerful forces that can move very quickly around the globe. You can make a lot of progress toward your strategic objectives with your Navy, especially with fast-moving carrier groups and battleships. You can use their far-ranging strike capabilities in a short amount of time to really make some offensive progress in a lot of situations. But the Navy has to have safe ports of call to refuel and resupply, so if a fierce ground fight is raging, they may have to pull back to friendly ports, thus giving up those great offensive gains from time to time. Likewise when the economy pulls back and we go into recession, U.S. stocks don't hold the kind of ground that bonds potentially can. In that sense, the navy is much more capable of projecting force and, thus, it is offensive in nature. Within the Navy, we have amazing capabilities such as submarines, carrier groups, frigates, battleships, and all sorts of diversified forces. There is a similar variety of capabilities within the category of domestic stocks. We have small capitalization stocks, intermediate capitalization stocks, and large capitalization stocks, which are terms that refer to the overall size of the company's market value. Then within each of these size classifications you have different industry sectors such as technology, consumer discretionary, utilities, materials, energy, financials, consumer staples, health care, and industrials. Each of these categories of stocks has different capabilities and characteristics and will behave differently in various market conditions. For example, when the economy is doing poorly, consumer discretionary stocks may not do well since consumers are not likely to spend money on things like new jewelry or golf clubs. But utilities may do well in that same market environment because most people will still pay the power and gas bill, even if they can't afford discretionary items. You can see that even though American-based companies are considered domestic stocks, there is a lot of diversification that can be done within this asset class. Therefore, when it comes to our asset allocation, we're not going to just put some of our money into the Navy; we'll instead try to further diversify within that asset class. We'll make sure we choose a great mix of submarines, carrier groups, frigates and even Navy SEAL teams to allow us to have a force that is using all of these unique strengths to accomplish our mission. Can you imagine the reaction if the Secretary of the Navy recommended that the entire Navy be focused on only aircraft carriers? People would think he had lost his mind, so don't do that with your investments either. Work with your advisor to select the right mix of domestic stocks for your mission.

Air Force

For the Air Force I see a direct connection with international stocks. Much like the Navy, the air force can get places very quickly and project enormous force capabilities throughout the globe—in some cases even more quickly because they've got long-range bomber, surveillance, and other capabilities under their command. So the Air Force can really reach out to far-away places and get things done. For example, in many conflicts, the air force is able to wield great effects and get much of the job done through air superiority, which can reduce or eliminate the need to commit ground forces. They also have the ability to be defensive in nature by fending off other air forces, but they're not particularly good at holding a large amount of ground or keeping insurgents out of villages with large presence patrols. In that same way, international stocks can get a lot done for your portfolio by growing very fast at times—typically faster than U.S. stocks—but they also tend to be more volatile. They've got great offensive capabilities, but they're not going to be quite as defensive as bonds when the economy hits a rough patch and the markets falter. But we still want them in our portfolio because of those great offensive characteristics; we just have to allocate the right portion of our defense budget so they complement our other branches. Like the army and the navy, the air force is also very diverse in that they have many different capabilities such as long-range bombers, fighters, and close-air support. One of those close-air support assets is the A-10 Thunderbolt, which is very good at quick, dexterous maneuvering needed to engage ground forces. The A-10 is also called the Warthog, but many people refer to them simply as tank killers because they have a 30-millimeter Gatlin-type cannon on them that can destroy a tank very efficiently. Capabilities like this enhance the overall strength of the air force, but you can clearly see that there is a wide variety of very unique capabilities within the branch itself. The same principle holds true with international stocks available for your portfolio. There are developed countries like Japan, Germany, and France that will have completely different growth patterns and volatility from emerging market countries like Brazil, Russia, India, and China. Then, if we take that a step further, each of the industry sectors that exist within domestic stocks, such as utilities, consumer staples, energy, and so on will also be present in each country around the globe. A utility company in Germany may perform very differently from a utility company in India, for example. So when you meet with your secretary of defense, make sure you seek strategic diversification within international stocks, just as the air force seeks to maintain a strategic array of capabilities that make it the envy of militaries throughout the world.

Marines

The United States Marines are a good parallel for discussing the overall asset class known as alternative investments. Although definitions vary, the term *alternative investment* is generally used to describe investments other than traditional stocks and bonds. This includes investments such as hedge funds, commodities, real estate, precious metals, and other tangible assets. I think this is a good analogy because the marines are great at being the first to fight in a tough situation. They can make a big difference in very dangerous combat missions because they're tough, aggressive, and committed to victory. I've seen them in action and, believe me, the Marines have earned my respect. But there's a little joke that if someone needs to be knocked on the head, you call the marines; if someone needs a hug, you don't. When it comes to investing, alternative investments such as hedge funds, commodities, and real estate have a similar mindset. They are much more aggressive and volatile than other asset categories and can make you a lot of money, but you had better balance them out with other investments to reduce the overall risk of your portfolio. You might have oil, gold, or silver that goes through the roof in one market environment and comes down hard in other environments. Investments such as commercial real estate or farmland can have wide performance swings as well. Just as it is with the other branches of service, you definitely want to have a few good marines on your side, but they should not be the only part of your portfolio. Although they're extremely good at what they do, you may not want them handling your grandma's fine china. Instead, let them bring their strengths to the fight alongside your army, navy, and air force, and together you'll have a portfolio that you can count on to fight and win the battle to reach your strategic objectives, no matter what challenges you face.

As you can see, as the president for your financial country you have some great forces to choose from, each with distinct strengths that can help you achieve your mission. Your job now is to work with your secretary of defense to select the asset allocations that have the best probability of accomplishing your strategic objectives.

Build Your Armed Forces with a Mission in Mind

Your financial advisor will use your strategic objec tives and mission to help you allocate your resources to your Army (bonds or fixed income), Navy (U.S. stocks), Air Force (international stocks), and Marines (alternative investments).

KEY TASK 1: Work with your secretary of defense (financial advisor) to develop an asset allocation for the investment accounts you are using to fund each of your objectives.

At this moment we are focused on developing your asset allocation with your secretary of defense, but I want to remind you about where this step should fall in the process. Once you've identified your strategic objectives in Chapter 7, you'll then sit down with your cabinet and clearly communicate those objectives to ensure a unity of effort. After you have assessed all the risks and benefits, you'll need to allocate your resources to each of these cabinet departments, making sure that you have met all *Combat Finance* minimums discussed earlier in the book. Once you have allocated to each of the other cabinets and built your reserves, your ongoing spending on your department of defense should be a minimum of 10 percent of your gross income, as we discussed before. Finally, since you chose an outstanding secretary of defense in Chapter 6, he or she is going to help you create a world-class military to accomplish your missions.

Having said that, I want to talk about some of the pitfalls I have seen over the years so that you are more prepared when you meet with your secretary of defense. This first one is going to sound really obvious, yet people do it all the time: Don't put too many eggs in one basket. A good example of people who didn't take this to heart are the folks who put all their retirement savings into their own Enron company stock. When Enron went under, they lost everything because it was all allocated not just to one asset class (such as the navy), but also to one stock (all submarines). Say it together slowly for emphasis: S O U P S A N D W I C H. On the other hand, if people who worked at Enron had a diverse 401(k) that wasn't heavily focused on their own company's stock, they would be relatively unscathed by the effects of their company's collapse. Sure they would have to look for a different job, but their 401(k) would have still been intact. And if they were *Combat Finance* readers, they would have their reserves to cover them while they were in transition.

What would you think of the Secretary of Defense if you turned on the news and saw a feature about how he scuttled all tanks,

Humvees, ships, aircraft, Bradleys, and everything else to put all the nation's resources into the Coast Guard because he feared an attack on our shores. Or if he put the vast majority of the nation's military might into a new type of armored Batmobile-type vehicle? Or if he said that because the air force had done so well in the last few years of conflict that the United States was going to scrap the other three branches of service? You would think that was insane. And it would be, so don't make the same mistake with your own finances.

KEY TASK 2: Review your asset allocations in detail at least once a year when you conduct your full annual review with your cabinet. Adjust as necessary at each review.

In the last two chapters, you've built your cabinet and solidified your strategic objectives, and you have just met with your secretary of defense to allocate your armed forces. All of that is highly important, but you are not finished. Now you must sustain this process by regularly reviewing your strategic objectives and meeting with your cabinet to make necessary adjustments. There is a lot of debate within the industry about how often you should do this, but I believe that a good place to start is with a comprehensive annual review. If you have a major life event between annual reviews, then by all means gather your cabinet and make the necessary adjustments, but as a general rule an annual review is about right. It is frequent enough that you can keep your strategic objectives on track, but not so frequent that you get into the habit of obsessing about your plans. It's easy to build an annual review into your calendar and thus more likely that you will actually stick to it, which is half the battle with anything that requires discipline.

At your annual review you should clearly communicate any updates to your missions and desired outcomes, such as gifts to heirs, or donating to a church or alma mater. This will allow your secretary of defense to help you plan for that by raising the necessary cash ahead of time. Then you won't go to him right when the markets are down and it's a disadvantageous time to pull those funds. And although this is just an example of the types of issues that might come up, if it were your issue you would want to be sure to communicate with your secretary of state, your attorney, so that he or she can advise you on the best way to give that money away. Maybe that's in a family LLC or through a charitable remainder trust, but your attorney is going to be the expert in that realm. All of that needs to be done in direct coordination with your secretary of the treasury, your CPA, to make sure that you're doing it all in the most tax-efficient manner. So the more that you communicate your objectives with your cabinet in your ongoing discussions, the more you ensure a unity of effort toward your desired end state.

One way of doing that, which I encounter with some of my best clients, is to do a family meeting with the CPA, the financial advisor, and attorney. Having that meeting once per year is ideal. And, yes, you'll pay an hourly rate for your CPA and your attorney, but in my opinion it's a small price to pay for the value of clearly coordinated efforts. If you go in with a solid agenda, you'll know exactly what you're going to discuss, and you can be in and out of the meeting in less than an hour. Every time I've had this kind of meeting, it has led to discussions on things that could actually improve the client's financial, tax, or estate planning situation. It also sets the tone that you expect your cabinet to communicate and work together to accomplish your objectives, and that has an incredibly powerful impact. There is a difference between value and cost in this situation. This will cost you an hour or so at your CPA and attorney's rates, but don't confuse cost with value. If you show up prepared, you will come out ahead despite the cost. One tip is to meet at the attorney's office because she's probably the highest hourly rate, so why pay her to drive across town?

No Two Armed Forces Are Alike

Unfortunately, it's impossible for me to tell you exactly how to allocate your resources in *Combat Finance*. In fact, I'd be irresponsible if I did, because we haven't met to discuss your specific situation. However, I can tell you that your armed forces should be well diversified and designed to meet your objectives (but only you and your cabinet know what those are). There is no one proportion of army to navy to air force to marines that is right for every nation, just as there is no one-size-fits-all solution for financial asset allocation. That's why you need to build a solid cabinet and hire an extraordinary secretary of defense to help you develop one for your financial nation. Only you will know which strategic objectives and missions you chose to war-game in Chapter 7. Only you will know what timeline to operate on for your retirement age. Only you know how many kids you will put through college and how much you'll contribute to that mission. All these things have a dramatic impact on asset allocation.

Even if your family is very similar to another, your asset allocation may still be very different. For example, let's take two families, each with two parents and two kids who are the exact same age with the same amount of time to retirement. Even with all of these similarities, the asset allocation isn't always going to be the same. For one thing, each family will have a different risk tolerance, and an experienced financial advisor will ask a lot of questions to figure that out. If one of the families is going to really worry and possibly even begin thinking about selling every time the market dips, then that family needs a completely different allocation from a family who sees market pullbacks as an opportunity to buy. The family that sees the pullbacks as a buying opportunity is probably going to make more money on their investments over a lifetime, but there is nothing wrong with the other family's feelings about the market, so long as they allocate their portfolio to accommodate those risk-adverse feelings. So you must be brutally honest and truthful with yourself and your advisors when it comes to assessing your risk tolerance so that you and your secretary of defense can pick the allocation that is actually right for you. Otherwise, you may find yourself wanting to go to cash in a down market or make other emotionally driven decisions that can do real harm to your long-term portfolio return. Good financial advisors will understand this and be more conservative with their funds to avoid losing their trust, so take the time to find a good advisor that puts your needs and concerns first. There are also factors like income and inheritance that will have a big impact on asset allocation decisions. For example, if one family makes $200,000 per year and receives a $2 million inheritance, they're probably going to allocate much differently from the other family who has no inheritance and makes $50,000 per year. That family with an inheritance might be able to invest in high-grade municipal bonds and other safer instruments and still meet their goals, whereas the second family may need to be much more aggressive to get the kind of returns they'll need to meet their retirement and other financial goals.

With all these factors that come into play, you and your advisor must determine a specific allocation that is right for you and your circumstances. If someone tells you that she can come up with an allocation for you without understanding you and your family's goals completely, you're not talking with the right person.

One of the biggest things I see derailing people from achieving financial success is that they spend hours upon hours upon hours trying to decide which stock to buy. Earlier in my career I had clients who had hundreds of thousands of dollars of cash, and they were always on the precipice of deciding which stock to buy, but they never did. Had they simply focused on running their business and being the most productive they could be in their chosen career and allowed me to do my job as their secretary of defense, they would have a much more effective operation. They selected me to run their cabinet, so they know I'm competent, but they're too busy trying to pick which rifle to add to their collection than remaining engaged in the bigger picture. Over time it cost them dearly in missed opportunity and wasted time and effort. As the president of your financial nation, you need to use the mission statements that you developed in Chapter 7 to communicate your strategic objectives for retirement, college savings, and travel, and then allow your cabinet to use their expertise from there. They need to make those operational decisions to allow you to focus on the big picture. Allowing your secretaries to take charge and win that operational war for you is more effective.

The dominant narrative on the news is always going to be about what's hot. And that can be entertaining. But does anyone at any of these outlets know your personal mission? No? Therefore they don't have the information necessary to recommend something to you that would be effective in accomplishing your personal financial mission. You need to build armed forces that can meet your objectives. Anything else is a gun collection.

After Action Review

If you have finished this chapter successfully and have completed the following tasks, you are hereby promoted to Command Sergeant Major E-9 (CSM) in *Combat Finance*. You have:

1. Completed and maintained all key tasks from previous chapters.
2. Consistently followed your *Combat Finance* general orders.
3. Consistently maintained your financial bearing.
4. Completed your consumer debt pay-off plan from Chapter 1 and remained debt free.
5. Calculated and built your reserves as described in Chapter 2.
6. Used the battlefield calculus described in Chapter 3 to budget for, save and purchase a home that you can defend in the face of financial attacks.
7. Established retirement savings of *at least* 10 percent of your income and made it automatic through payroll deduction or an automated weekly or monthly bank transfer.
8. Analyzed your insurance needs and purchased the prescribed minimums in Chapter 5.
9. Carefully developed your cabinet, using Chapter 6 as a guide.
10. Turned each strategic objective into an actionable mission statement:
11. Built your armed forces:
    a. Developed an asset allocation for the investment accounts you are using to fund each of your objectives.
    b. Established a plan to review your asset allocations in detail at least once a year with your secretary of defense.
    c. Established an annual review plan to communicate changes and updates in your strategic objectives to your full cabinet.

If you have not completed each of the key tasks in this chapter, *continue reading,* but you are barred from promotion until you meet these minimum standards.

Chapter 9

Why We Fight

There aren't many people in this world who are willing to fight in harm's way without a motivating factor that drives them to succeed. What makes people join the military when they understand the risk of being deployed? What makes a firefighter run straight into a building while others are running out? It's not that these folks want to be deployed to a dangerous foreign country or voluntarily go into a dangerous blaze. Those who join the military believe in fighting for the freedoms that they and their families enjoy. Firefighters know that they must protect their community. They do it because they believe in something bigger than themselves.

After navigating the *Combat Finance* journey, you should also have a concept of why you are fighting for your financial future. I'm pretty sure that ultimately, you're not doing this just for a bigger bank account than the guy next door. You're doing this for at least one motivating, emotional, personal reason. You're doing this because it gives you and your family the financial freedom to accomplish their dreams and goals and aspirations. These dreams may not be monetary, but having your financial future secured allows the nonmonetary goals in your life to become reality. A solid financial future means less stress, feeling balanced, better health, and stronger relationships with family.

Make a Difference

After returning from my deployment to Afghanistan, I thought about all the things that happened in theatre that made me completely reassess my life and priorities. It was a tough year. I began to take stock of my experiences and some of it was negative. One of the most indelible moments was the death of Specialist Brandon Steffey along with his bomb dog, Maci, on October 25, 2009. We had seen a surge of IED activity before winter, and Steffey and Maci had just been assigned to help our unit. The single worst day of my life was when they were caught in an IED attack and I escorted their bodies from Laghman to Baghram. Later that year, I had to secure the scene after one of our sergeants was stabbed to death on the FOB. It was a horrific image that I won't ever forget. Losing these two people during my time there, as well as the overall experience of that year abroad, galvanized my belief that I had to do something positive to try to dull the negative.

SPC Brandon K. Steffey with Maci

Killed in Action, Operation Enduring Freedom, Laghman Province Afghanistan, October 25, 2009.

I was lucky enough to bring back a daily reminder of how we can all overcome adversity. I met Aimal Halim when he was assigned to work with one of the units on our FOB as a translator and cultural advisor in Afghanistan. Aimal and I immediately hit it off, and we talked about his life: how his father died when he was six months old, leaving him and his mother to work every day to put food on the table and get clothes on their back. Aimal worked long hours as a translator, but he talked often about doing something more with his life, to change his family's fate. So I made him a promise that if he came back to the States to pursue his education, I would find a way to help him make that happen, including supporting his mother while he was studying. Aimal came to the states shortly after our 221st Cavalry with a student visa in hand. He is working toward a bachelor's degree in political science at University of Nevada Reno and expects to graduate in 2014. He provides me with endless inspiration in life and in my financial work, a constant reminder of making the best of the situations we're given. I feel so deeply that trying to help others like Aimal is the way that we can turn so many negatives into positives.

Aimal and Afghan Religious Officer

Good people stay with good people. Aimal is proof that good people can be found everywhere in the world, from all backgrounds and religions.

We can make a difference not just in our own financial futures, but in the world. While I was deployed in Afghanistan, I saw what real poverty looked like, and it changed my perspective when I got home. My identity was no longer caught up in the things I had or the car I drove. I think that's one of the lessons that I try to convey to my financial clients: It's great to have things if you can afford them, but your identity can't be tied up in them. Put your time and resources into what's important to you, not an image that you think others care about. The ironic thing is that if you concentrate on what is truly important and don't live to impress others, you're more likely to achieve your goals, and that will impress others. One of my favorite sayings is that success happens when preparation meets opportunity. If you follow the process laid out in *Combat Finance* you will be prepared to help someone like Aimal. Or you'll be ready when your daughter gets accepted to law school or when your dream house comes on the market.

When I was a young lieutenant, I was at Gowen Field near Boise, Idaho, for an annual two-week training exercise. It was the second-to-last day, and we had gone through our exercises and put all the tanks and our weapons away and decided to go see *Braveheart* at a theater. Anyone who has seen the movie knows about the oversized, breathtaking scene at the end when William Wallace is being tortured and yells, "Freedom!" at the top of his lungs. Every one of us filed out of the sold-out theatre in silence, blown away by the enormity of the film. I immediately looked at my friend and said, "Let's go kick some ass!" The 40 people within earshot all began laughing, probably because we all felt the same energy. We were all revved up to go out and fight for something worthwhile. It's that kind of feeling you need to have at the end of this book. You'll never entirely end your *Combat Finance* journey, but you will need to end your journey through this book by feeling invigorated and ready to go kick some financial ass.

It's time for you to revisit what invigorates you on your financial journey. Do away with the feelings of being overwhelmed. Feel excited, instead, that you're about to secure your family's financial future and that you're going to move closer to achieving your dreams. Look at what you've learned about so far: basic training, building reserves, securing your FOB, training with Sergeant Major, protecting the home front, building your cabinet, turning your strategic objectives into mission statements, and building an armed force. You should be proud. You should be confident. You should be fired up and ready to continue your journey.

It's time for you to not just embrace the principles in *Combat Finance*, but to take immediate action toward your goals. Remember what Patton said: A 90 percent plan aggressively acted upon today is better than a perfect plan tomorrow. Some of my clients say that they don't want to think about or talk about money. They'll even go so far as to compare financial planning to going to the dentist. Not talking about money is a great way to go broke. The problem is that if they don't do the planning necessary to set themselves up for financial success, they'll spend more time worrying about, talking about, and thinking about money than if they just went through the *Combat Finance* process from the start. Look at people who don't pay attention to financial matters. These people will commonly have personal strains and pressures that others don't—in their home life and at their jobs, and elsewhere. Don't be so financially stressed that you have to worry about it each day. Instead, take the steps in *Combat Finance* seriously so that you can live your life with confidence.

Nothing Worth Doing Is Easy

Part of the *Combat Finance* process has been about learning how to take the bad with the good. There are going to be bumps in your financial road. It's not always going to be a rosy path. But by sticking to the principles you learned in this book, these bumps in the road won't be anything you can't get through. Know that these bumps are part of the process. Use these challenges to drive yourself, and know that if you stumble you can start or restart your *Combat Finance* journey at any time. You're never too old or too young to dedicate yourself to this journey. Follow my process, and you're going to win in the end.

There are many people who weren't initiated into the processes of investing and financial responsibility the way you are now. Some people have never faced a financial hardship and wouldn't know how to make it through that challenge. And still other people have never faced a financial windfall. I had a client once who received nearly a half million dollars in a settlement. She didn't build that money herself and didn't truly understand how difficult it is to do that from scratch. Immediately, friends and family started to come out of the woodwork asking for money. I sat down with her and talked about this and how to say no, yet she depleted the money to nearly nothing within a year-and-a-half. I told her over and over how withdrawals of anything more than 4 percent per year would deplete the value over time, but she continued to withdraw money from the principal, and soon there was nothing. She didn't have an understanding of what an incredible gift of lifetime income that money could have provided, and she didn't have the propensity to say no to people who asked for it. She didn't have *Combat Finance* values instilled in her, and the money was gone forever.

But for the number of people who haven't tried to live *Combat Finance* values, there are just as many who do. Early in my career, one of my young clients was making $75,000 per year as a contractor. For his age it was a lot of money, and he acted like there was no tomorrow. He would blow thousands on a trip to Las Vegas; he went to strip clubs and bought new cars. As time progressed and he became a father, I saw the light bulb go on. He now consistently enjoys his salary, but he also puts 10 percent of it aside to invest for the future. He learned the value of *Combat Finance* principles by not living them and making mistakes, but recovered using his modified behaviors. People do grow and mature. I don't care if you're 20 or 60, or what crazy things you did in the past; if you start handling your finances better today, then you're going to be better off in five years than you would be otherwise. Take action today to start the process to get yourself on track.

Ben Franklin once wrote in his essay, *The Way to Wealth*:

> Friends, the taxes are indeed very heavy, and, if those laid on by the government were the only ones we had to pay, we might more easily discharge them; but we have many others, and much more grievous to some of us. We are taxed twice as much by our idleness, three times as much by our pride, and four times as much by our folly; and from these taxes the commissioners cannot ease or deliver us, by allowing an abatement. However, let us hearken to good advice, and something may be done for us; God helps them that help themselves, as Poor Richard says.

I think that's a great saying because it means that we pay so much more in taxes for our own idleness and unproductive sloth. You're going to sit around and watch TV and sit around doing things that cost more than any tax ever does. You'll do things for pride, like buy an expensive new car or truck, and you'll make mistakes on bad investments. But it's the people who get up and do something right now, who work hard on modifying their behaviors today rather than tomorrow that end up making the most progress. Check your compass often on your financial journey, and you'll learn to navigate your finances and stay on track.

One of the most important things I can leave you with is the concept of the Officer Education System and the Non-Commissioned Officer's Education System. These education systems in each branch of the military are a way of helping you learn about what your superiors do, so that you are ready for positions of greater responsibility, which is a vital element of the growth and development of the profession. By learning the job of the person above you and teaching your job to the person below you, the military is building a system and unit that is larger than any one individual. As such, we try to always place the long-term good of the unit above our own career or aspirations. Some people think that they are great leaders if their units or teams collapse without them there. This is hogwash. The sign of a great leader is that he or she has trained their subordinates so well that they can step away and the engine will continue to hum along without them as though nothing has changed.

So, too, must an investor pass on knowledge to the next generation. A good commander understands this and prepares junior leaders to take the reins one day. It's your last key task in *Combat Finance*: to transfer to your children or someone younger not just wealth, but the wisdom to manage wealth in the long term. That means not giving your kids an open checkbook whenever they want it. That means showing your children how to stow away 10 percent of their own earnings (even their allowance). That means allowing them a window into your own processes for saving, spending, and budgeting. Discussing the costs and benefits of financial choices and then bringing kids into the decision-making process at an early age enriches their lives infinitely.

This kind of education also helps kids make it through the hard times when they face financial adversity. *Combat Finance* isn't about obsessing over the bad, but working toward a future with the understanding that the unexpected does happen. Understanding the bad times doesn't make unhappy kids; it makes kids who are happier because they aren't crushed by every challenge that comes along. This whole process comes down to one thing: What do you want to leave behind when you're gone? Your legacy will be augmented by the values, behaviors, and strategies you've put into place during your *Combat Finance* journey. Do you know what is truly important to you? Allow *Combat Finance* to guide you there. If it means downsizing your life so that you have more time with your kids, make that happen. If it means switching careers to what you really love to do, despite the paycheck, then do it. This book is for the every man and every woman who wants to learn how to accomplish great things from small beginnings.

If you've read *Combat Finance,* then at some level you want to change. What made you want to change? Reach down, look inside, and figure out what it was that caused you to pick up this book. The worst thing you can do is to get excited about *Combat Finance* and then do nothing with that energy. You have all the incredible potential in the world to do what you want with your *Combat Finance* knowledge. All you need to do is take the first steps. Imagine your life in a few years: debt free, with reserves, and a plan for investing in your future. Imagine how great that will feel. Take action now to become the financial warrior you want to be. Nothing to it but to do it.

Afterword

Lessons Learned

Well, *Combat Finance* readers, as we say in the cavalry, it's been a great ride. I hope that this journey helped you pick up some of the values and discipline that will help you and your family to achieve financial freedom. Since today's training is coming to a close, it's important for us to look back at what we have learned and to keep those lessons close at hand. All great military units and championship teams review lessons learned to help make them better in the next fight or the next game. I know you are going to be a financial champion, too, so we're going to review the key lessons learned in *Combat Finance*. Soldiers put checklists and smart cards in the battle book that they keep in their cargo pocket or close at hand to reference when needed, and I want you to do the same thing with the key lessons learned in *Combat Finance*.

Combat Finance Lessons Learned

- **90 percent of success is right place, right time, right uniform, right gear, and right attitude**
  - *Focus on the things you can control first. Then worry about the other 10 percent.*

- **A good plan aggressively executed today is better than a perfect plan next week.—Patton**
  - *Don't worry about or wait for perfection. Take aggressive action now and adjust along the way.*
- **Soup sandwich**
  - *You're better than that.*
- **Nothing to it but to do it**
  - *The maximum effective range of an excuse is zero meters.*
- **Maintain your financial bearing**
  - Self-discipline is easier when you have systems in place.
  - Emancipate yourself from the spending expectations of others.
    - *Structure your life and your attitude so you make good financial decisions. Don't listen to friends or family members who are pressuring you to overspend.*
- **The *Combat Finance* General Orders:**
  1. I will work diligently to be the best that I can be in my chosen profession and constantly strive for improvement.
  2. I will proudly accept the responsibilities that I have to my family, my community, and my country, and I will perform all my duties in a professional manner.
  3. I will maintain my financial bearing by living within my means and purchasing only what I have earned, while consistently investing a portion of my income to improve my future.

DO NOT forget your *Combat Finance* general orders. Post them where you will see them daily.

Principles of Financial Freedom

- **Live within your means**
  - Know what you make.
    - *You control this by focusing on general order 1.*
  - Know what you spend.
    - *Be honest about needs versus wants.*
  - Pay off your debts.
    - *Building wealth cannot be achieved without this step.*

- **Build and maintain reserves**
  - Operational
    - *Complacency kills—Willfully operating without reserves is dereliction of duty and a great way to get you and your family hurt.*
  - Strategic
    - *Sun Tzu—Every battle is won or lost before it is ever fought. Prepare now to win that future battle.*
  - Tactical
    - *Remember your battle drills, SOPs, and load plans so you can strike when opportunity presents itself.*
  - Bad news is not fine wine; it does not get better with age.
    - *When the enemy strikes, don't live in denial. Accept the situation as it is, tell the family the truth, and work together to fight through tough financial challenges.*
  - Be the sea captain with steady pace and voice.
    - *Reserves allow you to keep your wits about you when the financial cannonballs are flying.*
- **Choose your FOB wisely**
  - Your home (FOB) has many benefits, but it is also a liability.
  - 20 percent down to avoid PMI.
  - Total payment with taxes and insurance <35 percent of take home.
  - 15- or 30-year fixed. No ARMs.
  - Larger homes have larger taxes, utilities, and maintenance.
    - *You cannot win the war from inside the FOB, so remember your battlefield calculus and leave plenty of income free to invest outside the wire to win financial victory.*
- **Learn to love training**
  - Last season's training won't win this season's championship.
  - Invest a minimum 10 percent of monthly income. More is better.
  - Start now and utilize the power of compound returns.
    - *The time value of money can work to your advantage.*
  - Make investing automatic.
    - *The best discipline is easy discipline.*
  - Take advantage of employer matching; it's free money.
    - *You wouldn't walk by a $100 bill. Pick it up!*

- Make use of automatic deductions at work.
- Set your bills and investments to automatically pay.
- Never go to battle without a plan.
- The harder you train, the luckier you get.
    - *You always find a way to do the things you love, so learn to love investing 10 percent* ***or more*** *of your income every month. If you do, luck will find you.*
- **Protect the home front**
    - Life insurance—Minimum 10 times annual household income for breadwinner/minimum 5 times for non-breadwinner.
    - Health insurance—Never go without.
    - Disability insurance—60 percent of income for all earners until 65.
    - Long-term- care-insurance—Evaluate as you near retirement.
    - Renters insurance—If you rent, get it.
    - Home and auto insurance—Higher deductible is cheaper.
    - Establish a will or trust for all adults in the family.
- **Understand the value of advice**
    - Seek wisdom and avoid overconfidence.
        - *We don't know what we don't know, so seek advice.*
    - Select your cabinet
        - *Seek advice and referrals from the wisest people you know, not your broke buddy or high-spending uncle.*
    - Secretary of defense
        - *Your primary financial advisor.*
    - Secretary of state
        - *Your attorney.*
    - Secretary of the treasury
        - *Your accountant.*
    - Secretary of homeland security
        - *Your insurance agent.*
    - Czars
        - *Your real estate agent, hair stylist, florist, and so on.*
- **Turn your strategic objectives into mission statements**
    - The fundamentals of planning
        - Strategic objective: a primary goal, such as retirement or college expenses, whose success is necessary for the individual's or family's overall vision to be realized. Goal or just objective for short.

    - Mission: A clearly articulated assignment, generally intended to achieve or help achieve a larger goal or objective.
    - Mission statement: Clarifies the objective or goal and describes how it will be accomplished by articulating who, what, where, when, and why.
    - Purpose: The broader reason for which a task is being undertaken. Explains why we're participating in this mission.
    - Key tasks: The mission-critical steps necessary to reach your desired end state. If key tasks are not completed, the mission will fail.
    - End state: The fairy tale ending. What right should look like when everything in the plan comes to fruition.
  - No commander willingly goes into battle without a plan.
  - Prioritize your strategic objectives.
  - Communicate your strategic objectives to your cabinet.
  - Use a mission statement to create unity of effort.
  - Delegate and review results regularly.
    - *You preside over your cabinet, but they run it. Stay engaged, but don't quit your day job. Establish an annual review process to stay on track.*
- **Build your armed forces, not a gun collection**
  - Start with your strategic objectives in mind.
  - Know what missions are needed to meet your objectives.
  - Design your armed forces to meet your missions.
    - *Build your financial army, navy, air force, and marines.*
  - Review your armed forces annually to stay current.
  - Focusing on what's hot at the moment will lead to a gun collection.
    - *Gun collections are cool to show your friends, but they don't win financial battles for you.*
  - Your financial nation is unique.
    - *Be honest with yourself and invest accordingly.*
- **Know what you are fighting for**
  - Keep a picture with you at all times of what motivates you. Your family, your dreams. Let that image drive you to succeed.
  - Make a difference.
    - *No one will ever remember the car you drove or the watch you wear. They will remember your character and how you affected their lives, for good or bad.*

- Nothing worth doing is easy.
  - *Take the good and bad in stride to reach your dreams.*
- A good commander teaches his job to the next generation.
  - *Teach what you have learned to the younger generation in your life. Your kids, your nephews, and nieces. Teaching them to fish is better than giving fish.*

- **Nothing to it but to do it!**
  - *It's worth repeating.*

Bonus Lessons Learned

I am blessed to have built some great friendships over the years, both in the military and in civilian life. As I get older and hopefully wiser, I have come to realize that it's best to listen to the wisdom of others and learn from them whenever possible. After all, I make plenty of mistakes on my own, so why not avoid a few by listening to the wisdom of others. During the writing of *Combat Finance* I asked many of my friends and family, colleagues from work, and former brothers in arms to share their ideas with me. Many of those ideas made it into the body of the book, but others just didn't for one reason or another, but they were too good to not share. The following are a collection of additional lessons learned that I think you will enjoy.

- **Several colleagues from work shared these gems about how to ensure that your secretary of defense has the *lowest possible chance* of helping you meet your strategic objectives.**
  - Keep your secretary of defense totally out of the loop when it comes to big financial operations you are planning.
    - *If you are planning a land war in Asia, you might want to let your secretary of defense know so she can help you plan.*
  - Surprise your secretary of defense with a phone call the day of a complex operation.
    - *You have been thinking about investing in some real estate, but rather than warn your secretary of defense so she can help rebalance your armed forces ahead of time and counsel you about funding options, spring it on her at the last minute so she's forced to sell at the mercy of the market.*

- Don't consult with your secretary of defense about the best way to conduct a military operation.
    - *Don't assume that your secretary of defense has never had a client open a new business or make a large real estate purchase. Rather than just spring it on her, call and let her know what you are trying to accomplish, and see if she has any ideas that you have not considered.*
- Refuse to discuss anything with your secretary of defense's chief of staff, even if it is about tasks that the secretary of defense will surely hand right back to the chief of staff.
    - *Your advisor's assistant is his or her chief of staff. Let him help you with all the paperwork, ordering of new checks, changing addresses, and so forth, so that your secretary of defense can focus on the fight to reach your strategic objectives.*
- Call your secretary of defense and tell her to start moving forces around the globe, from army to navy and from region to region, but don't discuss the strategic objective.
    - *Your secretary of defense is there to help you meet your objectives, so even if you have a strategy in mind, talk to your secretary of defense about what you are trying to accomplish and why you think the strategy you have in mind is sound. Then let the secretary of defense respond and hear her out, even if it's not what you want to hear. You can always continue on with your original plan, but at least you have heard other opinions on how to best accomplish the mission.*

- **First Sergeant B is one of the great NCOs I had the opportunity to work with while serving in 1-221 Cavalry. He shared two great lessons I think you should read.**

  "When I was serving in Operation Desert Storm we finally had a minute to stop after two hard days on the go. Everyone was tired and wanted to fall out. Some of the guys went to get chow. Others went to do basic tasks, but enthusiasm for details was seriously lacking as everyone felt entitled to a break. I settled in for just a moment, but then had the sudden thought that I needed to shave my beard in order to be able to maintain a seal on my protective mask. Tired and worn out, I reluctantly assigned myself the unpleasant task of a dry shave rather than take the few minutes of down time to relax. We moved out shortly thereafter and sure enough, just over the next hill, an M8 chemical alarm went off. Moments before I had to convince myself that a shave was necessary, but when I put my mask on and got a good seal I was never more grateful to have a clean close shave."

- *Outstanding lesson learned from the first sergeant. How many times will we get complacent about reserves, about insurance, about maintaining our FOB that is defendable because it seems unimportant at the time? But when the financial chemical alarm goes off, we'll wish we had a clean, close shave.*

"I have also learned to identify self-perpetuating cycles and break out of them. For example, if the enemy attacks a convoy with an IED, the first-order effect is to build better armored vehicles to resist the blast of the IEDs. The enemy then builds a more powerful IED, so we build a better V-shaped hull, and so on. This self-perpetuating cycle can only be stopped by expanding the vision of the problem, such as seeking out the bomb maker, identifying the source of the materials, and defeating the network as a whole."

- *Again, great stuff, first sergeant. So often, people find themselves in financial straits and their first thought is where to get some cash fast. Borrow from mom and dad or a friend, or even seek out a payday loan. But in reality the best thing to do is to figure out why you are short of cash in the first place. Are you maintaining your military bearing? Are you following your* Combat Finance *general orders? Have you reduced your expenses and built your reserves? It is only by addressing this complete system that you can solve the real problem and reach financial freedom.*

- **I consider myself fortunate to have completed my command having had several of the best Chaplains in the army serving with us. One of them, Chaplain O shared this concern for the soldiers he serves.**

  "As a chaplain, the two greatest issues soldiers face and are counseled on, generally speaking, are relationship and financial issues, and many feel completely overwhelmed by them. The Master Resiliency Trainers (MRT) teach soldiers what steps to take in proactively dealing with any situation life throws at them. I'm wondering what steps one can take to establish financial resiliency, that is, when they hit rock bottom and have to choose which bills to pay, have much debt, destroy their credit, and so on. Should they take money out of their savings account, still have a 401(k)? It seems like most live from paycheck to paycheck and many are part of the 'working poor.' How do people get back in the saddle (using cavalry lingo)? These are part of the life skills that many don't have, and it seems that many are in need of this type of financial counseling."

- *Chaplain O, thanks to you, your fellow chaplains, and an outstanding NCO corps, I have been well advised over the years about how often our soldiers and their families struggle with managing their finances. That is why I wrote* Combat Finance, *and that is why one third of the author's proceeds are going to the Combat Finance Foundation, whose sole mission is to provide financial education to our military members and their families. You can learn more about the Combat Finance Foundation at* www.combatfinance.com.

- **This lesson comes from one of my favorite air force officers, Major C.**

  "The air force *loves* its checklists. We don't fix an airplane, fuel a vehicle, or process an enlistment without an official checklist. Especially in the maintenance world, they're pages and pages long, but they serve to keep people from forgetting small items or overlooking exactly how to do something mundane. I'm a big list maker at home when it comes to my personal finances (and the rest of my life, ha, ha), and I often wonder if it's because I was exposed to the ease of tracking ability by making lists and checklists."

  - *Absolutely right Major C. Whether it's our monthly budget or establishing exactly what our operational and strategic reserve amounts need to be, if we don't write it down and track it, it will probably not get done. So use the budgets and checklists in* Combat Finance *to help you keep track and reach your goals. You can also go to* www.combatfinance.com *to download materials and purchase the* Combat Finance *workbook.*

- **I told you about one of my personal heroes, Shane Baldwin, in the Introduction. When I asked him what**

lesson he would share, he talked about the importance of having a battle buddy, as we call it in the army, or a wingman, as they call it in the air force.

"Buddy teams are vital to keeping each other safe. We all have a friend who's in trouble, or we need a mentor ourselves sometimes."

- *That's so true, Shane. In the military we know it's not a reflection of our strength or manhood to need each other on the battlefield, yet so many people back home think it's a sign of weakness to need a battle buddy to help them get through tough things like managing their finances. I, for one, respect a guy (or gal) who is man (or woman) enough to stand up and admit they need some help figuring it out. I hope that* Combat Finance *will help, but there are a lot of great resources out there for our military personnel. Ask your NCO or chaplain for help finding resources or go to* www.combatfinance.com *for help.*

- **This last one comes from Captain A, who works for a large international corporation. He and his coworkers realized one day that they were having the same kinds of conversations about money and other life problems, just the way they had with friends back in high school and college. But it became obvious that their problems had changed over the years as their careers progressed, and one of them captured a valuable lesson.**

  "Everybody has problems. Do you want to have poor-people problems or rich-people problems?"

  - *Don't think that if you just get your finances in order that all of your problems will go away. They won't, but you'll have problems like what kind of college fund to choose from instead of how you're going to pay rent this month. The road to financial freedom is a lifelong journey, not a race with a big banner at the finish line.*

Glossary

adjusted gross income (AGI) Total gross income minus specific reductions allowed by the United States tax code.

allons Motto of the 11th Armored Cavalry Regiment (ACR), which means "Let's Go" in French.

arsenal A stored collection of weapons or equipment.

asset allocation An investment strategy that balances risk and reward by distributing a portfolio across many different asset classes, including equities (stocks), fixed-income (bonds), cash, and others.

artillery Large-caliber guns used in land warfare.

B-hut A small, nonpermanent housing structure commonly used as shelter for troops in Afghanistan. They house about eight people and are often constructed with plywood. The name is rumored to come from the structure's impermanence, referring to B-grade housing.

balloon payment A repayment of the outstanding principal sum made at the end of a loan period.

basic training An initial period of training for new military personnel that involves physical training and intense behavioral discipline.

Bernie Madoff A former stockbroker and financial advisor who was convicted of operating a Ponzi scheme that stole billions of dollars from his clients and is considered the largest financial fraud in U.S. history.

blivet A large bag of water.

bonds A debt security in which the issuer owes the holders and pays them back with interest and principal. It is a form of loan.

cadet An ROTC or military academy officer in training.

capital gains A profitable difference between the higher sale price and lower purchase price that comes from the sale of an asset such as a stock, bond, or real estate.

carry As in "owner will carry the note" or "owner will carry the mortgage." The owner is willing to either finance the purchase for you or is willing to maintain responsibility for any existing mortgage on the property until it is paid in full. This usually occurs when the seller is highly motivated and the property is such that buyers may have difficulty obtaining traditional financing.

close air In military tactics, close air support is air action by fixed or rotary-winged aircraft against hostile targets that are close to friendly forces.

cockroaches Instructional technique in which the trainee lies on his or her back and puts arms and legs up in the air, moving them frantically like a dying cockroach until the drill sergeant is convinced that the trainee is adequately trained in the subject at hand.

consumer debt These are debts owed from purchasing goods that are consumable and do not appreciate in value. This is debt used to fund consumption rather than investment.

COP Stands for Combat OutPost, a well-fortified area used to house forces and engage the enemy.

draw One of the five key terrain features. A draw runs downslope from a saddle.

dividend A share of profits paid to the owners of a stock or other investment, usually paid at quarterly intervals.

drill sergeant A noncommissioned officer who instructs soldiers in military, tactical, behavioral, and physical exercises.

dying cockroaches See cockroaches.

end state The fairy-tale ending. What "right" looks like when the key tasks are achieved and everything in the plan comes to fruition.

equities A stock or other ownership interest in a company.

FOB Stands for Forward Operating Base, a secured military position that is used to support tactical operations.

goal A quantifiable outcome or achievement needed to realize a larger intent or vision.

gross income Total income before taxes or deductions.

hedge fund An aggressively managed portfolio of investments that uses advanced investment strategies in an attempt to increase a fund's value to the investor.

hooch Personal living space. Not to be confused with the drink, or the doctor on Scrubs (that guy is crazy).

IED Stands for Improvised Explosive Device, a commonly fabricated and lethal device designed to destroy a target, most often a military vehicle and its occupants.

infantry Soldiers who train to fight on foot with individual and man-portable crew-served weapons.

intelligence officer An oxymoron according to 97 percent of enlisted personnel, but also a staff officer who is in charge of enemy information collection and analysis for the unit commander.

interest A charge for a loan. Usually a percentage of the amount owed.

key task The mission-critical steps to reach your end-state. If these don't happen, the mission will fail.

KIA Killed In Action

little johnny hut A toilet shelter.

liquid investment Something that can be immediately accessed. Can be bought or sold quickly in large volume without affecting its market price. Such as a savings account or CD.

load plan A document that explains in great detail the arrangement of personnel and equipment aboard a vessel or aircraft.

low crawl An exercise in which a person moves along close to the ground. The torso goes along the ground, twisting and moving arms and legs while moving under wire, through mud or through a dangerous territory.

marksmanship Skill and accuracy in shooting.

M1 Abrams An American main battle tank. It is named after General Creighton Abrams.

M4 A magazine-fed, gas-operated, air-cooled, semi-automatic or three-round burst, handheld, shoulder-fired rifle.

MEDEVAC The evacuation of military or other casualties to the hospital in a helicopter or airplane.

military bearing The appearance, attitude, and conduct of a military member that brings respect to his or her branch of service.

mission A clearly articulated assignment, generally intended to achieve or help achieve a larger goal or objective.

mission statement Clarifies the objective or goal and describes *how* it will be accomplished by articulating "who, what, where, when, and why."

mortgage A legal document by which the owner (i.e., the buyer) transfers to the lender an interest in real estate to secure the repayment of a debt, evidenced by a mortgage note.

municipal bond A security issued by or on behalf of a local, county, or state authority.

MWD Military Working Dog.

net income Income in excess of revenue after taxes, depreciation, and other expenses.

NCO NonCommissioned Officer.

night infiltration Act or process of moving into hostile or unfriendly territory at night.

objective A quantifiable outcome or achievement needed to realize a larger intent or vision.

one "O" five rocket or 105 rocket. Soviet-built rocket commonly used by anticoalition forces in Afghanistan.

opposing force A military unit tasked with representing an enemy, usually for training or war-game scenarios.

outside the wire When a soldier is beyond the secure confines of a base.

Ponzi scheme A fraudulent investment operation that pays returns to investors from the flow of money from new investors rather than from legitimate profit earned by the underlying organization. Named after Charles Ponzi, who ran such a scheme in the 1920s.

principal The total amount of money borrowed (not including interest).

purpose The broader reason for which a task is being undertaken.

rappelling To descend from a height, commonly a rock face or wall, by using a rope.

realized capital gains Result from changes in the value of capital assets, such as stocks and bonds, between when they are purchased and when they are sold.

ruck A backpack-like sack used to carry equipment.

ruck march A long walk with a heavy rucksack. Often used as an assessment of physical fitness.

S&P 500 The Standard and Poor's 500 Index is a stock market index based on the market capitalizations of 500 leading publicly traded companies in the United States.

saddle A dip or low point along the crest of a ridge.

soup sandwich Term used to identify or bring attention to something that is not up to *Combat Finance* standards. Although it may refer to something that's messed up, disorganized, or unfinished, it is actually a way of saying, "You can do better than that. Try again."

stocks A type of security that signifies ownership in a corporation or a claim on part of the corporation's assets or earnings.

strategic objective A primary goal, such as retirement or college expenses, whose success is necessary for the individual's or family's overall vision to be realized. *Goal* or just *objective* for short.

success A natural state that occurs when preparation meets opportunity.

Sun Tzu A military strategist and philosopher from the Chinese Zhou Dynasty who is traditionally believed to be the author of *The Art of War.*

T-72 A Soviet main battle tank that entered production in 1970.

TACSAT Tactical satellite communications.

theatre In war, the theatre is the geographical area of the armed conflict.

thinking man position A plank-like exercise designed to both strengthen the core as well as ensure complete understanding of whatever the drill sergeant was saying.

unrealized capital gains An item or security not yet sold, so the gains have not been realized or made permanent.

About the Author

Kurt Neddenriep is a senior vice president of a major Wall Street investment firm, who began his career in January of 1996 and is a founder of the Mountain West Group. Kurt enlisted in the Nevada Army National Guard in 1990 as an infantry soldier to help pay for college. He commissioned as an Armor officer in 1994 and entered the investment advisory business after completing the Armor Officer Basic Course in Fort Knox, Kentucky Kurt gained a unique perspective on financial management by simultaneously pursuing his military career in the Nevada Army National Guard as he built his financial practice. The teamwork, integrity, and professionalism that he learned as a platoon leader, troop commander, and squadron commander of over 500 armored cavalry troopers has helped shape the Mountain West Group into an efficient and effective team that is process driven. The team model was successfully put to the test when Kurt deployed to Afghanistan from January 1, 2009 to April 2010. Kurt returned to a strong team that had survived the downturn with both client portfolios and client relationships intact. Kurt retired from the Nevada Army National Guard in February 2013 as a Lieutenant Colonel and began working on *Combat Finance.* His awards include the Combat Action

Badge and the Bronze Star Medal, both earned during his service in Afghanistan in 2009–2010. Kurt is active in his local community, having served as the past president of the Rotary Club of Elko and the Elko Boys and Girls Club board, in addition to supporting many other local boards and charities.

Associations

Allons Club Member, Blackhorse Association; National Guard Association of the United States; member and past president of the Rotary Club of Elko; member of the board emeritus and past president of the Boys and Girls Club of Elko; Paul Harris Fellow with Rotary International; served multiple terms on the board of the Great Basin College Foundation and Elko Chamber of Commerce; established Neddenriep Family Scholarship with matching donations from the Morgan Stanley Foundation and Barrick Gold Corporation, which provided tuition for dependents of Nevada National Guard Soldiers and employees of the Boys and Girls Club of Elko; 2009 "Twenty Under 40" by the Reno-Tahoe Young Professionals Network; Veteran's Guest House 880 Club Member; member of the Investment Management Consultant's Association.

Education

Bachelors of Science in Business Administration with a major in Finance and minor in Economics from University of Nevada.

CIMA® Executive Education from the Wharton School of Business.

Index